CARING

CARING

Experiences of looking after disabled relatives

Edited by
Anna Briggs and Judith Oliver

Routledge & Kegan Paul
London, Boston, Melbourne and Henley

First published in 1985
by Routledge & Kegan Paul plc

14 Leicester Square, London WC2H 7PH, England

9 Park Street, Boston, Mass. 02108, USA

464 St Kilda Road, Melbourne,
Victoria 3004, Australia and

Broadway House, Newtown Road,
Henley-on-Thames, Oxon RG9 1EN, England

Set in 11 on 13 point Baskerville
by Set Fair, London
and printed in Great Britain
by T. J. Press (Padstow) Ltd,
Padstow, Cornwall

Library of Congress Cataloging in Publication Data

Caring : experiences of looking after disabled relatives.
1. Handicapped—Great Britain—Family relationships—Case studies.
2. Handicapped—Care and treatment—Great Britain—Case studies. I. Briggs, Anna.
II. Oliver, Judith.
HV1559.G6C37 1984 362.8'2 84-15109

British Library CIP data also available

ISBN 0-7102-0332-2

Contents

The editors

Anna Briggs is in her thirties and has four children and one step-child. Active in the Women's Movement and working at one time for Age Concern, she began to work on the issue of caring as a neglected women's issue and a social issue of great importance. After leaving Age Concern she obtained a research grant from the Equal Opportunities Commission and eventually produced the Report *Who Cares* published by the Association of Carers. In 1982, her second husband, Brian Gallon, was diagnosed as suffering from cancer, and she moved from being one of the people who, with Judith Oliver, had worked to make caring a national issue, to being a carer herself 'at the statistically correct age of 35'. She has also written a chapter in the Virago publication *Walking on the Water: Women talking about Spirituality* (ed. Garcia and Maitland). She also helped Jo Campling collect some contributions for the RKP book *Images of Ourselves: Women with Disabilities Talking*, which gave her the idea for this book. She and Judith Oliver met after they had both been successful in getting media coverage for carers in the late 1970s, and formed the steering committee which led to the setting up of the Association of Carers. Anna has recently moved from her native North-East of England to the Island of Iona off the West Coast of Scotland, where, as members of the Iona Community, she and Brian are working on the resident staff of Iona Abbey for a time.

Judith Oliver is married to a tetraplegic. They and their two teenage children live in Kent. Judith started the Association of Carers as a response to the stresses of caring which she had seen in her work as a technical officer for the visually handicapped with Kent County Council, her contacts with voluntary organisations concerned with disability and in her own family. She has written extensively on the subject in journals connected with social work and community policies and was a contributor to *A Labour of Love: Women, Work and Caring* (ed. Finch and Groves, published by RKP).

Introduction

This isn't a book about statistics. The inspiration for it came from another book published by RKP, in which disabled women spoke about their lives and experiences. We decided that a book in which carers talked about their lives would also be invaluable, and would have two main purposes.

Firstly, it would speak to other carers, who are feeling isolated and vulnerable, and whose very mixed feelings about their situation often lead to intolerable burdens of guilt and depression. There is something both comforting and powerful in discovering that you are *not* alone, and that thousands of other people are experiencing the same degree of conflict, both in the demands being made on them, which they feel they cannot adequately meet, and in their emotional response to the caring situation. So this book is firstly addressed to carers, in the hope that if some carers speak out, and tell their own stories, it will encourage others not to bottle up their feelings, and to try at least to identify those aspects of the situation which give them most problems. In this way, they may find some ways of working these things out, of finding some solutions, however small.

Secondly, it would speak to those who have not experienced caring more than any amount of statistics can. Those who have not been carers or are not carers now fall for the purposes of the book into broadly two important groups. Firstly, there are those in the general public who may very well become carers at some time in the future, but who are now voters and members of organisations, trade unions, women's groups, churches, charitable groups, and so on, and who as such can have a say in the formation of policies which will assist carers. Too often we can find that those who shape policy are those who are not debarred from a great involvement in public life by what are seen as their private, domestic responsibilities. So it often happens that policy is formulated by able-bodied, 'economically active' people aged between about 25 and 60 years of age. The majority of policy formulators are also men, whereas the majority of those with domestic responsibilities have been shown to be women. If 'ordinary' people who are not carers but are voters in local and national elections, and are people who can pass resolutions of intent and mount campaigns through the bodies of which they are members, become enthusiastic about the cause of carers after they have matched up the increasing statistical evidence with the testimony of the carers in this book, it can only do carers good.

The other group which the book aims to address is that of what are now becoming known as the 'caring professionals'. Some carers are surprised, rightly in our opinion, that the word 'caring' is so easily claimed by a group who are in salaried work, with holidays, sick leave and pay, pensions, and so on, when carers themselves are having some trouble in establishing that they are in fact workers but with none of these benefits. Doreen Hore makes this point graphically in her chapter. But 'caring professionals' in the health and social services are supposed by the public in general to be the arm of the Welfare State which bears up and supports those in need. Carers have often found it difficult to impress on caring professionals just exactly what their needs and problems are. We have felt that, just as a day in a wheelchair is a salutary experience for an able-bodied person, so a day as a carer would also be a learning experience for those who have not been in this position. Far better still would be for those who seek to help carers to read carefully what the carers say in this book, to pay attention to both practical and emotional aspects of caring, and to consider how they may be contributing to the difficulties carers experience, rather than ameliorating them, in the forms of support offered and by the attitudes contained within those forms. We want to stress that by no means all carers are dissatisfied with services, but add that this may be a sign of the way they perceive the order of things. Instead of feeling grateful that the State in some form or another is assisting with 'their' problem, should we not aim for a society where dependent people of all sorts are the concern of all, and those closest to those dependent people can be assured of all sorts of support as they shoulder a disproportionate share of the community's mutual responsibility? The fact that it has taken us so long to get this book together is evidence that carers are unwilling to open themselves up for criticism by even *suggesting* that caring for a loved father, mother, spouse, sibling or child causes them problems.

It is worth stating at this point that this book, its sister book *A Labour of Love: Women, Work and Caring*, edited by Janet Finch and Dulcie Groves, and the growing pressure group, the Association of Carers, of which we (the editors of this book) are both part, is a response to a combination of circumstances which has made life harder than ever for carers in recent years. Though, as we said, not wanting to introduce statistics, we feel we need to stress what these circumstances are. Firstly, there is simply a vast difference in the sort of population we have today, compared with one hundred, fifty, or even twenty years ago. It has been shown by population statisticians that we all have on average nearly twice the life-expectancy of our great-great-grandparents, and at the same time are producing far fewer children. While more of the children we produce do manage to grow up, household size has continued to shrink, often catching planners and housing developers unawares. In the last century, many marriages ended with the fairly premature death of one partner, and the surviving partner often married again. Today people marry again after divorce, and so a 'family' is no more a stable unit than it was in the last century, for different reasons. Numbers of dependent people have risen through social and medical advance. People live longer, recovering from most infectious illnesses, and even permanently disabled children and adults (both physically and mentally disabled, that is) survive, with the aid of drugs and improved care and nutrition, infections which would have previously claimed their lives. The number of older people living to their seventy-fifth and eighty-fifth birthdays has risen quite markedly, and social planners have been warning for some years that, as a society, Britain (and other rich, Western nations) is not yet facing up to the social and economic consequences of this fact.

Many other social factors which seem on the face of it to have no relevance do in fact contribute to a worsening of living conditions for all but able-bodied, economically independent people. Amongst these we could include housing and transport policy, employment and education policy, health and social services planning, and the welfare benefit system.

Firstly, housing; this now reflects to a large degree the notion that a family is of the nuclear variety, self-sufficient, and geographically and socially mobile. In the public sector in particular it is difficult to persuade those who set standards that any other consideration is necessary other than that a family 'unit' is adequately housed in terms of rooms per person. The changing needs of people with increasingly dependent members of their 'extended' family is not usually seen as relevant – so it is a rare housing department which will rehouse a young family near an ageing relative or vice versa – even rarer the department which will arrange an exchange across boundaries for one or other of these parties. Even new private housing is rarely flexible enough to allow extra accommodation for an ageing or dependent relative to be added. Increasingly, too, residential housing is built outside town centres and assumes that the family has a car.

This brings us to transport policy. Two reports in the 1970s (1972 and 1976 PEP reports, edited by Myer Hillman) showed that those who have use of a car (as opposed to notional ownership in a family) are most often male, able-bodied and economically active, while those who have physical or economic handicaps more often have to resort to public transport. The reports claimed that there was an inbuilt bias in transport planning, in that, for one thing, journeys of under a mile were not counted, whereas these were in fact the majority of journeys for mothers of young children, older people, physically disabled people and children and young people. Many of the new estates, both council and private, are planned on the assumption that residents will have cars, but apart from the South-East of England, where two-car households are slightly more common, this planning overlooks the salient fact that when the economically active car-driver has left for his (usually his) place of employment, the rest of the family are car-less. Since the mid-1970s the public transport services in this country have suffered a decline due to government policy, and many people are left out on a limb where services were once good.

Education policy has also affected older, chronically sick and disabled people, especially in rural areas, as the closing of small schools has forced young families to move to market towns and larger centres, leaving in their wake older people either staying in the country or moving there after retirement. In many of these places, a couple who were retired may have owned a car, but on the death of a car-driving husband, a wife who has never learned to drive is stranded away from potentially caring relatives should she need help. Only a minority of women in Britain actually hold licences – of these it is arguable that many do not actually drive very often.

Employment policy also assumes that those seeking work can pull up their roots, and those of their nuclear family, and move to any area where there are jobs. This has resulted in great conflicts, when people are forced to leave behind ageing relatives; in recent censuses, areas like the North-East of England have been shown to have higher numbers of elderly people living on their own. As an Age Concern organiser in North-East England, one of the editors was often called on by sons or daughters who had rushed back from the Midlands or South-East in answer to a call for help from their mother or father, but who had to return within days or risk losing their job. A recent recruitment drive by the Department of Employment, in which out-of-work skilled manual workers were taken, free, to East Anglia, to be enticed by employment prospects there, gave a good example of how such employment policies completely overlook family responsibilities outside the nuclear household (never mind the connections that would be severed within the household).

It may be surprising that we have introduced health and social services planning as a factor in the worsening situation of carers. Few people are not grateful for life-saving and life-enhancing treatment from health services, or for the valuable support on offer from social services in certain circumstances. But however unintentionally, the rhetoric used to describe such provision has given the impression that informal, that is, family and neighbourhood care, became redundant in 1948. As many other critics have noted in much greater detail than we can here, health provision is often curative rather than preventive, can be accused of treating a patient, or their diseased organ or system, in isolation, taking little account of the home, family, and environment from which they have come and to which they hope to return – and in which their death will eventually be a significant event. So carers, often the next-of-kin to health service patients, will complain of lack of information about conditions, treatments and side-effects, and of their own needs and conflicting responsibilities.

Both in health and social services, support is often offered only on terms decided by the service providers, who make assumptions about the lives of those to whom they offer support which are based more on stereotype than reality. A carer's relief at being offered District Nurse or Home Help support may be tinged with frustration at being unable to know in advance when this support will arrive, so that her day's schedule, already difficult, is made impossible. An 'all-or-nothing' approach offers residential care on a full-time basis or not at all. Only recently, and especially in the field of mental handicap and child care, have institutions been proving they can be more flexible, and offer part-time relief.

In the field of benefits, many carers are caught in a 'Catch-22' situation, where their willingness to care results in financial penalties. Other researchers have shown the cost of caring for handicapped people in terms of lost employment opportunities and extra cost. If a carer takes an elderly relative into her own home, the relative may lose the rent allowance previously received, a heating addition, and other benefits related to her or his supplementary pension. Very little is allocated in tax relief to offset this loss. The most glaring example of dis-benefit is the bar on married women receiving Invalid Care Allowance. It seems to many to be more than coincidence that the largest number of carers cannot receive what is in any case hardly a generous benefit, but which carries other entitlements, such as pension credits. The welfare benefit system also proves slow to respond to changing patterns of care, so that in some circumstances, people lose Attendance Allowance, Invalid Care Allowance and Home Responsibilities Protection credits just because an institution proves flexible enough to arrange 'in-and-out' care for their relative (incidentally reducing the carer's burden from one of 24-hours-a-day, 7-days-a-week to something approaching the normal working week!). In our short portraits of carers, we have illustrated how some of these confusing policies affect real people.

All of these changing social factors provide an important backdrop to the stories told in this book – but they are only a backdrop. The most important aspect of being a carer is the emotional and psychological effect of changing roles and expectations arising from the inability of their dependant to be self-sufficient. Alongside the increasing longevity which most of us welcome has come a phenomenon unknown in previous centuries, which is therefore something that the human race simply hasn't learned yet to live with. The art of living with chronic illness and disability is something we have few patterns for. In former times people lived with the sort of debility from infectious and parasitic conditions which is suffered by millions in the Third World today, but few lived to acquire the variety of cancers, heart conditions, 'strokes' and degenerative illnesses which are the most common causes of death today. In years gone by accident victims, mentally handicapped people and sufferers from (usually undiagnosed) chronic and potentially terminal illnesses, would have succumbed to infection at a fairly early stage. In short, we have to invent new ways to live with long-term stress, caused by the unpredictability and unpleasant manifestations of these conditions. The effort to invent these new ways is undermined by the popular myth that grew up along with the health service – that we could now all enjoy robust health to the day of our death. External factors, such as changing patterns of medical treatment, and professional mystification, also affect these emotional patterns. The roles and expectations in which we live, and in which we have learned to live as we grow up, suppose that we will be healthy and self-sufficient as we play these roles, after we have left a fairly untroubled childhood. Husbands and wives, daughters and mothers, fathers and sons, bring these expectations to their relationships, and we are left without patterns of living when those expectations are unfulfilled. This is why we think, as editors, that it has been hardest to persuade the relatives of accident victims to write for the book. The fearful shock to the structure of living which comes along with a head injury or spinal fracture is often so bad that the carer can't bear even to write about the emotional turmoil caused. In some cases it is no understatement to say that bereavement would have been easier to bear than the prospect and reality of caring for a surviving accident victim, whose whole way of life and personality may have been changed as a result of the injuries sustained. Of course the carer *is* in such a case suffering a bereavement of a very real sort but is supposed to be simply grateful that her or his loved-one's life was spared.

It has been hard, in fact, to persuade many of the carers who have eventually written for us, that it was possible for them to do so. One of those who initially agreed eventually wrote to decline the invitation, and has given us permission to quote her reasons. The writer is in her thirties, with two children, and nursing a former professional husband who is severely disabled with multiple sclerosis. She writes:

> 'I am sorry to say that I have not found time to write for your book – I did try, but the fragmentary nature of my day makes it impossible to concentrate for long enough. Another problem is that trying to put my experience into words is just too depressing and that is something which I try to avoid at all costs.'

This letter gives one clue to the reader of this book – a very important clue. It is a book which contains far more than appears at face value. The reader will have to develop the skill of reading between the lines. Some of our contributors are quite frank about the effect of caring on themselves. Others hardly mention themselves, and write about the predicament of their relative, which of course they were perfectly free to do. But it will take little imagination to envisage the carer's own life, even when barely mentioned. In fact, the absence of self-concern only has the effect of tugging even harder at the heart-strings.

We have tried to include carers with dependants of all ages and conditions in this book, and the effect of this is to show up the common plight of carers, despite the differences in those they care for. Michael Bayley, in his excellent study of mentally handicapped people in Sheffield, showed that carers had come, over time, to accept 'solutions' to the management of daily life which would not be at all acceptable to those without dependent relatives. He cited the case of a couple who would sleep apart, one sleeping with the mentally handicapped offspring (hardly a child, but a person in his twenties), the other sleeping alone, this being the only way that a good night's sleep for all could be ensured. When carers adopt such solutions, they sometimes fail to notice how much they have 'lost' and so they don't complain. But often such losses burrow underground, as it were, and show up in the carer's health, either during or after the period of caring.

This book is a manifesto of sorts. Carers are sick of hearing about 'Community Care' which often means themselves, single-handed. They are tired of being told that 'people don't care for their relatives any more'. And they are beginning to realise their numerical strength – one of the editors found in research in the North of England, that there were *more* carers than mothers of children under 16 in the sample drawn from a door-to-door survey. After the carers' stories we will suggest what could and what must happen in the near future if carers are to continue caring, often sacrificially, for those who are nearest and dearest to them.

RUTH COWLING

Ruth lives in Hampshire and cares for her mother and assists her blind husband. She sometimes speaks on behalf of the Association of Carers at events in her county.

I loved my mother. It was my fervent wish that, should she need to be cared for in her old age, I would be the one to do the caring.

At the age of eighty-two, Mother became disabled through a fall. She had broken her knee and, in spite of surgery, was left with an unstable knee joint. Mother's doctor told us that the condition would get worse and that Mother was no longer capable of living alone.

I had three married brothers who, for various reasons, were unable to take Mother into their care. My husband and I expressed our willingness to care for Mother, providing that the other members of the family would relieve us for short holiday breaks. This was agreed.

Mother's house was sold, and a 'Granny annexe' was built on to our house, comprising a bed-sitting room with attached bathroom, containing toilet, washbasin and shower unit. My daughter and son were aged thirteen and eleven years, respectively.

For a while, all went well. I cooked Mother's midday meal. She got her own breakfast and tea. I did her shopping and washing and took her wherever she needed to go – to church on Sundays, to a weekly women's meeting, and to the hairdresser and chiropodist when necessary. Without too much difficulty, I fitted in these extra tasks with my other duties of caring for my home and family.

When walking, Mother used a walking stick. With her free hand she grasped my right arm and leaned heavily upon it. As a result of this, I developed a 'frozen shoulder', a painful condition. The social services department then provided Mother with a walking frame. Thereafter Mother placed her weight on the frame, rather than on me. But the damage had been done. It was about five years before I was free from pain in my shoulder.

After about eighteen months, Mother had what appeared to be a slight 'stroke', just as she was about to make herself a pot of tea. After that I made all her meals, including the mid-morning coffee. This considerably restricted my movements outside the house.

Every time I needed to have a day out, either for shopping or keeping a hospital appointment, my husband had to take a day's annual leave to look after my mother.

Within about three years, arthritis developed in Mother's injured knee, and walking became much more difficult for her. She had frequent falls. I managed to get her up by manoeuvring a low armchair into a position behind her and heaving her up on to it. If the fall was severe, I sent for the doctor. Sometimes Mother's ribs were bruised, and that meant a few days in bed. On one occasion, I had to apply pressure to arrest bleeding from a cut on the head while my son phoned for the doctor, who came and stitched the wound.

With the increasing difficulty in walking, Mother became more and more confined to the house, and this made her irritable. Her irritability was expressed towards me. Sometimes I became exasperated and raised my voice. Then Mother would say, 'Don't shout at me!'

By the time Mother had been with me for four years, arthritis had also developed in her shoulders. I now had to dress and undress her. Unable to walk as far as the bathroom, she now used a commode, and needed more and more help. Getting to and from the commode became a painful, time-consuming business.

I was getting increasingly weary as I tried to care for Mother and also care for the family and look after the home. Cleaning of the house had to be neglected. Washing was a priority. The amount increased as Mother became incontinent of urine at times and occasionally incontinent of faeces. Shopping consisted of quick dash to the shops to get food. There was no time to linger, as one always had the thought that Mother might be needing attention.

I could not invite friends in as I was too weary to entertain anyone.

After the first two years, Mother became too frail to travel to relatives for holidays. So she went into a local authority home for two weeks in the year to enable me to have a holiday. Those breaks were wonderful, but it took time to unwind, and I was just beginning to feel the benefit when it was time to take up my duties again.

When Mother had been with me for five years, my husband, whose sight had been deteriorating gradually, was registered blind. He needed help, especially at mealtimes. Sometimes Mother would call for attention when I was helping my husband at breakfast time. He had to be ready when the taxi arrived to take him to work. So I had to decide whose need was greatest at that particular time.

In spite of his disability, my husband was a great help to me. Mother was particularly immobile in the evening when she was tired. Then my husband would help me to get Mother out of her chair, on and off the commode, and into bed.

Mother's mental condition began to deteriorate. I often had to read her letters to her over and again, as each time she insisted that I had not read them to her. Sometimes she decided that the pills the doctor had ordered were doing her harm and she could not be persuaded to take them.

I desperately needed some relief from my burden of caring, but I didn't know where to turn for help. I went to my mother's doctor, who suggested I contacted the Social Services Department. I did so, and was told that a day centre was to be opened shortly in our area. When the centre opened, Mother was offered a place for one day a week. She went for a short while. It didn't solve my problem, however, as it was only open from 11 a.m. until 3 p.m. and, as Mother refused to go by ambulance, I had to take her and bring her back by car. Then she became too unwell to go there any more.

When the social worker for the blind visited my husband, she told us about the Attendance Allowance, for which she was sure my mother would qualify. So I made enquiries, and eventually my mother obtained the allowance. If we had known about it earlier, Mother would have obtained it sooner and I would have qualified for an extra year's Home Responsibilities Protection of my pension.

About this time, my mother was having difficulty in controlling her bowels. This entailed a tremendous amount of extra work for me. I sometimes had to give her an all-over wash including her hair, a complete change of clothing, and then wash the surrounding area of the room. This might happen at any time of the day, but it was particularly unfortunate when it clashed with the time for preparing the family meal. Mother's doctor arranged for the district nurse to visit and sort out the problem. For a while after that the district nurse visited weekly.

My mother had now been with me for six years. I was feeling completely exhausted physically, so I went to see my doctor. He advised me to contact the Social Services Department as my mother was not a medical problem. The social worker to whom I presented my case the next day was sympathetic. He told me that 'shared care' was sometimes available, the elderly dependant spending one month in a local authority home, and the next at home. He explained that, before he could take any steps in this direction, my mother's consent would have to be obtained. Mother refused to give her consent.

Then Mother had a fall and I could not get her up again. I rang the Health Centre and was told to ring for the ambulance. Two ambulance men arrived and helped Mother up into her chair. The district nurse arrived later and suggested that I asked the doctor to visit. When the doctor came the next day, I told him of all my problems with my mother. I expected some help, but he merely wrote out a prescription and said that I was to send for the ambulance whenever my mother had a fall and I could not get her up.

The following day my mother was very poorly and lapsed into semi-consciousness. She remained like this for several days. Everyone, including the doctor, thought she was going to die. The district nurses helped me to nurse her, coming twice a day. Mother recovered, but she was more immobile than ever. A nurse now came to blanket bath my mother once a week, thus relieving me of one task.

A few weeks later, I again told the doctor of my difficulties in caring for my mother now that she was so immobile. He arranged for her to be admitted to hospital with a view to increasing her mobility.

Mother's stay in hospital was an unhappy one. I was told that she was refusing all treatment. No doubt she was being awkward, but I was very unhappy about the general attitude of the staff towards my mother. After a fortnight, Mother was discharged from hospital. I was then told that she had been in assessment ward. I asked for an interview with the geriatric specialist. This was refused. Eventually, he spoke to me on the phone. He said that my mother had been assessed as not needing hospital care. He advised me to contact the Social Services Department. So we were right back to square one.

The social worker again told me that my mother's verbal consent would be necessary before 'shared care' could be arranged. Two weeks later one of my brothers visited Mother and managed to persuade her to give her consent. He pointed out to her that this arrangement was essential for my health and, without it, I would not be able to care for her at all. I passed on the good news to the social worker and he rang me a few days later to say that 'shared care' would be available. The date he gave for its commencement was *five months ahead.* So I struggled on for another five months.

It worked well. I was able to relax and recuperate during the month that my mother was away. The next month I was able to carry on, fortified by the knowledge that relief would be coming soon. My mother, when she was away, was more contented because she knew that she would soon be coming home again.

This arrangement continued for the next eight months. Then Mother was admitted to hospital again for rehabilitation. Arthritis of the spine had immobilised her still further and she was suffering a great deal of pain. She died in hospital, three weeks after admission, following a 'stroke'. She was nearly ninety years of age.

Looking back, I see that what began as a pleasant duty became an intolerable burden, and I was not able to convince those who had it within their power to help me that *I really had* reached the point where I could no longer cope single-handed with the task of caring for my mother.

Our society expects a woman to care for her dependant twenty-four hours a day, seven days a week, for fifty weeks in every fifty-two. I believe that our society is expecting too much of the carer.

NORMAN THODY

Norman, from West Sussex, cares for his wife, with multiple sclerosis, and son, who has cerebral palsy. Norman left his job in insurance to establish the Disabled Housing Trust, which has provided housing and care in purpose-built bungalows in Burgess Hill.

My wife Barbara and my son Grahame are both physically disabled. Grahame is now 21 years old and has been handicapped since birth. He is a spastic. Grahame is a bright, cheerful and intelligent youngster. He may have severe physical disabilities but mercifully he has good average intelligence. Barbara, now 42, has multiple sclerosis which was first diagnosed some seven years ago.

We had always wanted a child and I was delighted when Barbara told me she was pregnant. It was until the last moment a perfectly normal pregnancy. Since Grahame decided to exit feet first at the last moment it was felt advisable that Barbara should have him in hospital instead of at home. Everything that could go wrong with the delivery went wrong. Grahame was delivered with the umbilical cord wrapped around his shoulders. During his birth he suffered lack of oxygen which resulted in severe brain damage.

I shall never forget that week. It was thought our son would die but against all the odds he pulled through. He was a pathetic bundle and to start with he couldn't even suck or cry. I remember being told by the hospital that it might be better if he were to die, and even if he were to live he would be nothing but a living vegetable. Some vegetable!

The next year was harrowing for us all, Grahame had found his voice and never stopped crying; every feed took about two hours to finish. This was a testing time for us for other reasons. The prognosis from Grahame's paediatrician was gloomy and distressing. He was convinced our son would be severely mentally retarded but in time would be able to walk. During the following two years we became convinced this diagnosis was incorrect.

If I have a criticism of the medical profession it is their reluctance to take parents into their confidence. I found our discussions with them very frustrating. They are inclined to use words capable of different interpretations so that you could never nail down the problem. When we suggested that our son had a normal intelligence this was very strongly rejected.

Ultimately we were able to prove the original diagnosis to be wrong but it took us five years to do so. The actual prognosis proved altogether different. Grahame's intelligence is about average but he has severe physical disabilities. He cannot walk, or control some of his limbs and will always have speech difficulties. On the other hand he has had a college education, can use a computer, word processor, and operate a CB radio.

The years while Grahame was growing up taught me a great deal. You have to fight for your child and if you are articulate and intelligent then you are likely to succeed in getting the best out of the state system. What is so alarming is that the odds are stacked against most disabled families.

I am fortunate in having a wife of great courage and fortitude who was a devoted mother to our son. We may be guilty, as so many parents of handicapped children are, of being over-possessive but at least we were able to provide Grahame with a secure and loving environment in which to grow up.

Before Graham went to college Barbara had been complaining about an inability to co-ordinate her limbs, tingling, and other sensations. She was getting tired very quickly and seemed to have little energy. Characteristically she kept most of these symptoms to herself to spare me anxiety.

Eventually there came a time when these symptoms could no longer be ignored. She was referred to a neurologist who told her that she was suffering from neuritis but not to worry she hadn't got MS! The day after the consultation our GP rang me to tell me the truth about her condition. Yes, she did have Multiple Sclerosis but her consultant felt that it would not be in her best interests to be told. For four years I kept this dreadful secret.

Grahame was still at college but I knew that when he came to leave that drastic changes would have to take place in the life of our family. I concluded that in time I would have to give up my own business interests and stay at home to look after my family. I was then a successful business man who had started two insurance companies from scratch. I possessed a good income but I knew this would disappear when the time came for me to give up my work. I decided to save and invest wisely so that at least we should have sufficient capital to live on. Our standard of living would never be quite as high but it would be adequate.

Barbara was gradually worse and this culminated in a major attack in 1979, which put her into hospital. The episode itself was alarming, she had overnight become paralysed in both legs and arms. At the time Grahame was due to come home from college for the long summer holidays. I still had a business to run which I was then trying to sell, and this required my constant attention. I appealed to Social Services for help only to be told that there was nothing practical they could do. All they did was to give me the name and address of a commercial agency who might be able to provide some living-in help. In the end we got by but I swore then that this would never happen to my family again. For me this experience brought sharply into focus the inadequacies of the existing domiciliary services.

We had Grahame's future to consider, especially what would happen to him when he came to leave college. He could not be considered for open employment and in our large rural county there was not one single sheltered workshop or even a day centre within reasonable striking distance. It was suggested that we put Grahame on the waiting list for an institutional placement. We took Grahame along to see one of the establishments suggested. I shall never forget his reaction.

He found the place depressing. To him it was like a hospital and his college education had inspired and motivated him to demand more from life than this. Living in an institution was clearly a non-starter as far as he was concerned.

For my part I never could see myself solely in the role of caring 'house hubby'. I needed another challenge. My previous experience had impressed upon me just how vulnerable our family was. I was determined to keep our little family united and secure but just how could this be achieved? The state had nothing to offer, sheltered housing for disabled families where help was available to cope with emergencies or periods of stress simply did not exist.

I needed to take stock. I did, after all, know something about business, money and administration. A cruel twist of fate had provided me with a unique knowledge and experience. Could I not turn this to good account? My son's concern for his future coupled with my family's vulnerability were matters of great concern to me. Neither would be solved by recourse to the state. From these negative thoughts an idea grew in my consciousness. I felt what was needed by disabled families were sheltered housing projects providing accommodation specifically designed to meet the physical needs of disabled people, but more importantly where there would exist a supporting neighbourhood care scheme that would bring with it the essential security that would enable families to function. I had to convert thought into action.

So, before I gave up my business career I had established a charity known as The Disabled Housing Trust. Today we have built seventeen bungalows for families. We have care staff who respond flexibly to needs of our disabled residents. We are about to build a further twenty-four flats to give any disabled people who want to live in the community the chance of doing so.

If I have learned anything about caring it is to recognise my own vulnerability and limitations. Carers are valuable people, they save the state by their own personal sacrifice a great deal of money. In our project we try and help the carers in our families just as much as we do our disabled residents. For myself I have been fortunate in having a family who have supported me with a most ambitious project.

It is they who have provided the inspiration and motivation for what has been achieved. Arising from the tragedy of our personal circumstances we have been enabled to help others. This in turn has provided me with a real purpose to my life for which I thank God.

PAT HENTON

Pat is from East Anglia but now, in her early forties, lives in the North-East with husband Ken, a computer programmer. She cares for the daughter of their marriage, twelve-year-old Vicky, and has three older children, who live with her former husband. Vicky has been suffering from progressive mental handicap since she was a few months old and the cause of this handicap has never been fully determined.

Vicky is 12½ and profoundly handicapped, with a mental age of about five months. She is doubly incontinent, bottle fed and can only eat minced food. She is unable to play with toys or sit up without back support, but thankfully she is small for her age, weighing only three stone. Vicky is my husband Ken's only child, I have three from a previous marriage, they are 24, 22 and 18. They live in Norfolk, we are very close and they are really good with Vicky, I stay with them in the summer and they help with bathing, feeding and changing her.

That all paints a rather bleak picture but it's not as bad as it sounds, she is very pretty and very responsive, although she can't speak, her eyes and smiles say it all. She is able to laugh, watches mobiles, likes musical toys and loves watching television. She also smiles when she hears a piece of her favourite music. I enjoy looking after her most of the time. When she is ill, and she often is, I tend to get very low, always expecting the worst, the prognosis is rather bleak. The day-to-day caring, when she is well, isn't too bad. I have osteo-arthritis of the spine and lifting can be painful and difficult, but I try to avoid doing things I know are painful. My husband gives Vicky a bath and washes her hair on Sundays, and she has her hair washed at school mid week. I asked if it could be done as Ken works away from home quite often. We are lucky, he is in a well-paid job as a computer consultant.

We don't have a social life really, I choose to stay in with Vicky most of the time. Occasionally when she's in hospital we go out for a meal, and if something special is on Vicky goes into hospital overnight. We are very lucky with our paediatrician, if I ever feel I need a break she can go into hospital almost at a moment's notice. I find that knowing I can have a break whenever I want, I don't seem to need one too often.

Ken and I don't mind the change in our lives; we are in our early forties and are happy staying in most of the time. At the moment he's doing an external mathematics degree, so he is busy in the evenings when he's at home. We try to have a holiday without Vicky every two years, but we have lots of weekends and holidays in Norfolk with her. My family all live there, we live in the North-East of England and Ken's family live near, but as his mother is disabled and a widow and we rarely see his other relatives we are very much on our own with Vicky. Our marriage has been under a strain several times in the past twelve years. When we were first told about Vicky's handicap she was fifteen months old (I knew something was wrong but I didn't want to be told). I couldn't accept it, she was five before I came to terms with it and up until then I was taking valium, librium, etc. and took four or five overdoses, it was a very trying time for Ken. My older children lived with us until ten years ago when I had a nervous breakdown and Ken and I separated for a year. He had Vicky, I was unable to look after her. I feel really guilty about that and it still hurts just remembering. I sometimes feel we don't need each other now, he is very involved in his work and degree, and I centre my life around Vicky. I don't know what I will do with my life when she dies, I haven't worked for over twenty-five years, my home and children have been the centre of my life for so long. Vicky will leave a void I will never be able to fill. Life will go on, it has to; I'll find something to do. I'd like to go back to Norfolk near my children but it will depend on Ken's job. We've lived here for eight years because the school and hospital are so good.

We try hard not to be a handicapped family. So often a whole family thinks they can't do things other families do. I went through that when Vicky was much younger, I wouldn't take her out, all the nappy changing and feeding were awkward, I manage much better now yet she's so much bigger. I used to find myself apologising because she was handicapped, then I stopped feeling sorry for myself and got on with living.

Vicky goes in the car a lot and enjoys travelling, she likes going to school, her face lights up when I put her in the taxi and she recognises people she sees regularly. The school is a very good one; the atmosphere is always welcoming and friendly. Parents are encouraged to visit whenever they want. I often pop in when I'm out shopping. I have to do the heavy shopping when Ken is able to take me in the car. Vicky has to come too but she seems to enjoy the noise and bustle and all the people around her. I am unable to drive because I am epileptic through an injury twenty years ago, but I am controlled with drugs. Vicky is epileptic too; her fits are more difficult to control but she hasn't had a grand mal for eighteen months, we're really pleased about that, it's much easier to take her out in her wheelchair. We had great difficulty with wheelchairs until the Variety Club of Britain bought one for her. It's really nice, it has a thermal cover which is ideal in the winter, and a large shopping bag on the back. It's very stable even with heavy things in the bag. I have difficulty taking it out when the pavements have frozen melted snow on them, I tend to stay in more and live on food from the freezer.

I will always look after Vicky at home. She is regressing, but I will always manage somehow. I love her dearly and couldn't consider residential care. I have a reasonably happy life, I enjoy cooking, cleaning, knitting and sewing. I don't really have any close friends, I don't make friends easily, but I'm happy doing what I do. I don't always like being alone when Ken is away but it's part of his job and has to be done. We have happy holidays with and without Vicky – for a week or two I can be Pat, not Vicky's mum. It's nice for a week or so but I'm always so pleased to come back to her. I cry when I leave her but I'm all right when I get away. The nurses at the hospital are our friends. We've known some of them for eight years, so Vicky is never with strangers, and she's in hospital, ill, often enough to be used to it. When she's there, I sit with her from 10 a.m. until 7 or 8 p.m. and I do it because I want to. I love Vicky the way she is and wouldn't want her any different. If I need help I usually get it. I am able to go to the hospital and say I need a rest and Vicky goes in for a few days. I still sit with her all day but she's not my responsibility and I think that's the really tiring part in caring for someone you love, you feel so responsible for everything that happens to them. I feel very guilty when I am unable to cope or if I have to ask for help because so many people are in a much worse position than we are. I rarely contact my social worker, it's only when I need a piece of equipment. At the moment we are waiting for social services to install a shower. We've been waiting for nine months but these things always take time. I could manage Vicky in a shower but not lifting her in and out of the bath. It's lifting and carrying her that I find most painful. When my husband is away I sometimes have to ask a neighbour to carry her up to bed, he's always happy to do it. Having her has made me much more tolerant and I try to understand other people's problems more. We all have problems, they are just different in each family.

The three of us usually go somewhere for lunch on a Saturday, it's my day off! When we're in Norfolk Ken always gets Vicky washed and dressed in the mornings so I have a break, and he enjoys doing it. When he's at home he feeds her at teatime and puts her to bed, he always plays with her then. On the rare occasions when I'm ill and have to stay in bed he is quite able to look after us both, he can cook and is as helpful as anyone in his situation can be. I am able to get out as often as I want when Vicky is at school, so I'm only confined to the house when Vicky is off school ill or the weather is too wet or cold to take her out.

Over the years things have improved a lot, there is more back-up help for carers. Ten years ago I felt so alone, but maybe I cope better now. If I could turn the clock back thirteen years, knowing all the worry, heartache, tears and fears we've had and the sorrow still to come, I would still have had Vicky, the joy outweighs the anguish and she's been such a pleasure and delight to all of us who know and love her.

VAL HOLLINGHURST

Val lives in Sussex with her husband and two sons and her elderly mother who has had a stroke but she takes an active part in the Association of Carers and church work.

A 'tangled web' of emotions

One of the hardest problems I have found in caring for my mother has been coming to terms with the 'tangled web' of my own emotions: love, which naturally grows when you tend someone in need, mixed in with fear, resentment and guilt. Exhaustion and isolation made it difficult in the first stages to get anything into proportion or to make any effort to improve things.

When my mother had her stroke, 4½ years ago, I was just becoming established in my career as a teacher and a lay magistrate. After years willingly given to my family (two sons in early teens plus husband's career and home needs) it was now my turn to be a person in my own right. To find, quite literally overnight, that I had to give up the mental stimulus, the company of professionals, my ambition, to go back into the home and wash and care for my mother, was at least as horrifying to me as any more conventional redundancy.

The first six months were a nightmare. My mother's physical condition improved quite rapidly, but, to my horror, I found she had an almost total memory loss; she couldn't wash, dress, feed herself or do anything for herself, not because of the partial paralysis, but because she had forgotten how to. My mother had become my brain-damaged baby! My doctor's cheery 'You're coping marvellously. You don't need any help, do you?' was intended as a compliment, but it successfully cut me off from all sources of information and support – and without adequate information and people to talk to, fear takes over. Everyone needs help and information in the first stages if they are to do the job properly. So many of us make our own problems that wear us down later, simply because we don't understand the situation. It is no use either just asking whether the carer needs help or has any questions. I was too ignorant to ask intelligent questions or even to know what help was being offered, and I hadn't the courage to say so. It is not surprising, therefore, that I made just about all the mistakes possible. Most of these seem to be tied up in our image of what the world expects of carers. I saw myself as a cross between Florence Nightingale and an early Christian martyr – nursing and caring for my mother, keeping the home spotless, washing, ironing, cooking, shopping, gardening, yet always available with a sympathetic ear and practical help for my husband and sons . . . and of course, always smiling bravely! Fortunately, my marvellous family and friends pointed out that this desire for perfection was a recipe for a nervous breakdown, and I was forced to re-examine my new role and my reactions to it – a process I have not yet completed.

To begin with I had to recognise that I am not, and never have been, perfect, and secondly that if society really does expect such perfection from us then society is wrong. Anyone who criticises can take over for a month and discover reality the hard way. None of us are the superhuman people we would like to think ourselves and WE OWE IT TO THE PERSON WE CARE FOR TO LOOK AFTER OUR OWN WELL-BEING. This is not really a revolutionary concept – we service our cars regularly; who are we to think we can manage with less attention? All too often we feel that some professionals regard us as service units that will keep going with only an occasional pat on the head. Attitudes are changing, largely due to the efforts of the Association of Carers, but it is a slow business and in the meantime we must try to make sure we get some rest and refreshment, for if we break there may not even be someone to *visit* our relatives. With this and a knowledge of my own shortcomings in mind I started again. My family have learned from painful experience that I am a rotten nurse; but I am a good teacher, so why not try to teach my mother to care for herself? People do it for brain-damaged babies, so it should be easier for an adult who only has to relearn. The months of endless, patient repetition that followed were exhausting. When I could regard it as a professional job it was easier to cope, but when I remembered my once brilliant mother and watched her spending a week to do a 20-piece jigsaw puzzle I shed many a tear in private. But it was worth all the tears and anguish, because as she learned to do more and more and more for herself so her dignity as a human being returned and I can think of nothing more important than human dignity. You hear of someone who does everything for their disabled relative and society praises them – rightly if they have reached the stage where any movement or decision is impossible, but most people can learn to do *something* for themselves and it would be cruel not to allow them to make choices even if that does involve taking risks. Life is a risky business, after all. We don't wrap our children up in cotton wool and refuse to let them cross the road; we teach them to do it as safely as possible and then stand back. Why then do we try to shelter our elderly people from every wind that blows? The risk I found hardest to take was to leave my mother alone. Shopping was done in a frantic rush and all invitations out were refused. It was bad enough to risk my mother falling while I was unavoidably out, but the ultimate sin was to risk her falling *while I was enjoying myself!* Yet in the long run she gained by my occasional absences. A doctor's prescription saying 'Take time out to enjoy yourself at regular intervals' would often be much more valuable than valium. The first time I plucked up the courage to leave my mother at lunchtime I stupidly left her a Thermos flask of hot food – not the most sensible thing for someone who could only use one hand! Yet when I rushed back, instead of disaster I was met by a triumphant mother who had gone out alone for the first time and got help from a neighbour: she wasn't going to miss her lunch! My mother's confidence grew from that day on so we both learned from my mistake. We were both becoming people in our own right instead of prisoners locked together in mutual dependency and resentment.

There was still a long way to go. Humility has never been my strong point, and I found, still find, learning to accept help very hard. I have only recently realised that by doing everything myself I was depriving my mother of new friends, faces and experiences and making her far too dependent on me. Getting her to go to clubs in the first stages, though, was even harder than persuading reluctant toddlers that school was a lovely place really. 'I'm just a burden to you' is the usual response, but my *mother* is not a burden: the *illness* is a burden that we are both fighting together. It is amazing the difference it can make in a relationship when you define things accurately. Communication is just as important between carer and cared for, as it is between husband and wife. Elderly people often become very demanding, but how much of this is our fault because we shield them from reality? They probably don't realise that their demands are unrealistic and if we don't tell them we are encouraging them to be selfish. I now talk to my mother about my tiredness, my fears and needs and our love has increased with understanding. We don't let our children become selfish because it destroys friendship and ruins their lives in this life and the next. Do our elderly parents not have friends or an immortal soul?

Recognising that my mother and I are still individuals and cannot live through each other has been the most important factor in freeing us from the more damaging aspects of caring/cared for roles. Guilt is not as strong since I have acknowledged my own inadequacies and my mother's right to make her own decisions – even her own mistakes. She recently fell in the shower, and well-meaning friends and professionals said, 'You won't allow her to take a shower alone again, will you?' Note that word 'allow'. Is that why so many of our elderly people become senile, because decision-making is taken away from them in the interests of safety? I *asked* my mother whether she wanted help and she said 'no' very firmly. I hope I won't feel guilty if she falls again, but will public opinion insist that I do? It's harder standing outside the shower biting my fingernails, but as we've taken reasonable risks together our fears have decreased. Coming back into the world has also helped: fear feeds on isolation and lack of information. The Association of Carers has also helped because there I am a person in my own rights: a carer, yes – but not *just* a carer. In our local group we discover we are not alone, and we are still people.

I have found resentment the hardest emotion to come to terms with, and every time I think I've won the battle I find little pockets of it left. Why shouldn't I have a career as so many people assume is a woman's right these days? But if I had my career I wouldn't have so many other things that I now value. Having realised that resentment was growing inside me like a cancer I decided to fight it. If Christ could wash the disciples' feet, am I really too important to look after my mother? I have the prayer of St Francis on my kitchen wall and I am trying to live by it: 'May I seek not so much to be consoled as to console, to be loved as to love' . . . it's hard, and some people would say I'm just brain-washing myself, but the point is it works! I have reached the stage where if I had the opportunity to go back and leave the caring to someone else and take up my career I would refuse the offer! Because I've been at home, my house has become a meeting place for young people, friends of my sons, whom I would otherwise have hardly known – and what a joy their company has been. I've gained valuable insight into myself and become a stronger person, above all I've come to understand and love all my family, including my mother, more. Caring can do that to you – if you let it.

Of course I'm still afraid of the future at times and I have days when I wonder why I do it. Don't we all? Basically, though it all comes down to choice: very few of us have any real choice as to whether we care for our relatives or not, we do have a choice what to do with the very real burden caring imposes. We can wear it on our backs for everyone to see and pity us, or we can use it as a stepping stone to something better. I wear mine too frequently on my back – all that sympathy is lovely to wallow in – but when I have the courage to be positive I glimpse a freedom and happiness I thought were lost. I haven't unravelled all the 'tangled web' of emotions yet, but I'm beginning to think it is an interesting challenge. In years to come will I think I've been lucky to have that challenge?

Mrs A. and her husband have a profoundly handicapped son. Last year, when he was twelve years old, he weighed 11 stone and Mrs A. damaged her back when lifting him. No statutory service was available at the time required – 7 a.m. in order to have him ready for school – so Mr A. had to give up work to help his wife. The whole family now lives on state benefits.

DAVID BROOKES

David B. was a maintenance engineer in the North-East until his wife had a stroke in her thirties . . .

Remember the time when . . .

We are in a candlelit Italian restaurant, a quiet table for two. Sheila and I celebrating her birthday. It's April 1983, and as she sits there beautifully made up, hair freshly done, wearing an evening dress it is hardly noticeable that the shawl round her shoulders is draped over the back of a wheelchair.

It seems a million miles away from that cataclysmic day in January 1978 when Sheila suffered a massive stroke. When I saw her lying in a hospital bed, left side twisted, face contorted out of shape, blind in one eye and unable to speak except occasional single words, my heart broke. Where was the girl I danced the nights away with at a night club? What had happened to that fun-loving wife and mother to change her into a mis-shapen thing laid in white sheets? Over the next seven weeks she regained some sight in her eye, some speech, although it was still difficult, but not much improvement in her mobility. Then came the day of her discharge.

'She can go home today' announced the Ward Sister. Hurray, I was going to get my girl back! But how do I cope? What do I need to know? 'You will need a commode', Sister pronounced. So out of hospital we came, one wife, one commode and no idea of what lay in front of us. I found that the physiotherapists had taught Sheila to get dressed, using only her right hand – but no one had bothered to teach her how to take her clothes off again, as she always had her lessons at ten o'clock in the morning. So we both had to begin a new life. I gave up my job as a maintenance engineer to give her the full-time attention she needed. She, in turn, tried to learn to live a life so different that at times she felt like a three-headed Martian.

We had literally to live day to day at that time, and only long sessions with a locum doctor, Dr W. and lots of information from the Chest, Heart and Stroke Association helped us accept the moods of depression and elation as normal at this stage. Friends sometimes called only to be turned away at the door, because Sheila could not face them, even though she had felt able to cope in the hospital.

Then came the day Sheila decided to try to put some make-up on! She had always worn make-up and felt naked without it, so we tried. Not easy with a face still slightly contorted and only one hand to work with. My skills at wiring up complicated machinery paled against the prospect of applying mascara, and Sheila, after two hours, achieved a fair resemblance to Coco the Clown. So we gave up for that day. But she has got it together now, after many hours of patience and practice with cosmetics. Plus a little help from Blutak. But that's another story.

Our first outing into the town was such a total disaster that we can laugh about it now. We set off complete with wheelchair (on loan from the Red Cross) and a shopping list a yard long. It is only about twenty minutes' walk into the town centre and the shops, but trying to manoeuvre a wheelchair clear of pot-holes, round lamp standards, and getting the chair up and down kerbs without actually tipping Sheila out made it take three-quarters of an hour during which Sheila started to shake violently. I found she was frightened of the lorries and buses roaring along the road. Much more frightening from wheelchair height, than when you are just walking along. We even hid in a side street for a few minutes till we got back our nerve to carry on. Into our first department store, shopping list at the ready, feeling thoroughly shaken by our ordeal, but triumphant that we had got there, only to find out that the passenger lift was out of order, and if we really NEEDED to go upstairs we would have to find a porter and use the goods lift. So we did, only to be asked by a rather irate supervisor how we got there because customers were not allowed to use the goods lift under any circumstances! We left hastily, clutching the one item on our shopping list we had purchased. Back home to nurse our bruised egos and wonder whether we would ever be able to go out again.

About this time, the emotional side of our lives came to the fore. We had had a reasonable sexual life together. I was trying to play nurse and lover not successfully at all. Sheila, only 37 when the stroke hit, was growing more and more frustrated. How could she maintain her mystique as a woman when her husband had to dress and undress her each day anyway? The reaction we got from various organisations and individuals ranged from 'How can a handicapped person even THINK of having a love life?' to 'Give her two painkillers and get at it'. The Family Planning Association sent a visitor to see us, but even they admitted they could not help much. Our answer now is that our antics may not be wild and fantastic, but at least we have a lifetime's free supply of condoms!!!

Today we can look back at our achievements and disasters – like the trip to London on the new 125 train, where we were treated like royalty. Or how we entered a top London hotel via the meat lift and kitchens (we do seem to be prone to trouble with lifts, don't we?) or even the time we were refused entry to a cinema because the manager was frightened Sheila would burst into flames. We were a fire risk! We have learned to deal with problems at our own pace, accept that there are some things that may be impossible at the moment, but we may work our way round them in the future. We still have our irritations like the death-slide ramp the council insisted on installing at our front door – far more dangerous than the twelve-inch step we had there before. Or the changing cubicles in the brand new X-ray department of our local hospital. The doors are not wide enough to admit a wheelchair. But essentially this experience had made us a team. It has drawn us closer together than many other married couples we know and for that at least we are grateful.

Oh! Here comes the waiter with our meal, poor man, we are going to work THE SWITCH on him. Just watch. Sheila had ordered the fillet steak, and I prefer the rump steak with mushrooms. When the waiter arrives I insist the fillet steak is mine, and he is too polite to argue. Sheila cannot use her left hand properly to cut the meat. The fillet is placed in front of me, and Sheila gets the rump and mushrooms. I cut up the meat into manageable size pieces while Sheila quietly tucks into my button mushrooms. Then we switch plates. Sheila can enjoy her meal while I get on with mine and no one in the restaurant even notices what has been going on. That's our little secret but it works.

The future! 'One day at a time, sweet Jesus' is our theme song. We have never worked so hard in our lives, but through the laughter and tears of the last five years my heart mended. We will make that trip to Spain that we planned in 1980 – one day – even if we have to wait till after I have got my Open University degree, but that's another story. Cheers, my darling, happy birthday. We both have earned our night out.

MAGGIE ADAMS

Maggie is in her thirties, and lives with Peter and three children, the second of whom suffers from mental handicap which results amongst other things in behavioural disturbance. She works as a research assistant and lives in the North-East of England.

There are five in our family – me, I'm thirty-six, Pete also thirty-six, Liam who is thirteen, Sarah who is twelve and Peter who is three years old. We live in a large and tatty (we think it's beautiful) terraced house in Newcastle, with the added bonus of a garden – a great asset I can tell you. I work as a research assistant, looking at child development in the community – a very enjoyable but demanding job. I'm only able to do this because of the good offices of Pete, who must be the most supportive man in the world caring for the house and kids just as much and doing just as much work if not more than I do. We both work from home, so this makes life a little easier – usually, that is, though it can create problems in itself. I trained as an SRN and worked for some time in a school for mentally handicapped children, so it almost seems I was hand-picked to have a handicapped child. It certainly helps practically though I don't think it makes much difference emotionally. I've been married previously and Liam and Sarah's dad spends a lot of time with them and this too makes caring for Sarah much easier and gives us more time to spend with Peter.

I must say that I am in a much better position than most to care for a handicapped child – partly because of my past training and experience but mainly because of the great support I get from family and friends. Even so I sometimes find it a bit wearing, so God help those in a less fortunate position.

Well, what's it like having a handicapped child? Not that easy to answer. What's it like having an ordinary child? There are difficulties and great joys in both. Having two ordinary kids and an extraordinary one it's easy to see the similarities as well as the differences and I suppose in some respects the differences are very great, but you don't notice that much until someone asks you about it. I suppose it's different having a child who is born with a handicap to caring for someone who has just become disabled after having been perfectly normal. You just get used to it with a child who is different from the start. All babies need feeding, changing, loving just the same and you just continue to do it. It's only when you see children of the same age – Sarah is twelve now – that the true realisation hits you. When Sarah was born she just seemed a beautiful baby like any other – the fact that I couldn't breast feed her because she couldn't suck and the growing realisation that even from a bottle she had difficulty feeding made me suspicious all was not well, but the Doctor told us she was fine and I accepted or half-accepted that. No one wants to believe there is something wrong with their child, do they? By the time she was two and not doing a lot, it was apparent all was far from well. She had no language but could smile and scream – could she scream! When she wasn't asleep she screamed, poor little frustrated thing. I could still have thrown her out of the window at times! She would shuffle around on her bum by this stage and one would have expected a normal child to be getting into mischief that way. But Sarah didn't, she just screamed. Finally I took her to the Child Development Unit. A wonderful place, I was told; they will help you. I was very encouraged by this. Great, I thought, someone might take some notice of me. You get to the stage when you think that it's you. That you can't handle your own child and that it's your own fault. Rationally I knew that this wasn't true. She was my second child. I was a nurse, had had lots of experience with children, and I was sure that Sarah was not developing properly, wasn't I? Anyway Child Development Unit here I come – wait for ages and eventually see the great Doctor. 'Well,' he says after a lengthy interview, 'she's very pretty, I should take her away and not worry about it too much.' I couldn't believe it. I did go away for a while but I came back again and this time fortunately was put in touch with an Educational Psychologist who was wonderfully supportive and helpful and gave me just what I craved, which was practical support, help, and a direction in which to work. Things got better.

I think practical support and help are the most valuable things which can be given to carers. We don't want to be told how wonderful we are, or patted on the head and treated like some mentally subnormal saint. We want practical help. We want the occasional break. No matter how much you love your child you want some time away from them, and I think this is not limited to a handicapped child but it is that much more difficult to organise with a handicapped child. Sometimes I get fed up with having to bath Sarah and change her and dress her every morning. Not often but every now and then I think 'Am I going to do this for the rest of my life?' I don't mind usually but sometimes it would be nice not to have to do it. Sarah is now generally very pleasant but she does have her moments – throwing milk bottles across the floor and lashing out at odd times are recent developments. It's difficult to know the best way of dealing with it because it's difficult to know what's causing it, and as she gets older the difficulties do increase. A small handicapped child is O.K. to the rest of society, even attractive (as long as they don't look too bad), but an older one – well that's a different matter. It used to bother me sometimes when we went out and Sarah used to throw a tantrum, but it doesn't have the same effect on me now. It does on others though, and they sometimes get embarrassed and hurt by her behaviour. However, I feel that Sarah has got the same rights as anyone else and should go out and enjoy herself, go to restaurants, the theatre, etc., just like anyone else, and if other people are embarrassed well that's their problem. The danger is that it would be very easy with a child like Sarah to never go out and do anything, but we try to live as 'normal' a life as possible getting Sarah to join in as much as she can, and it works. Sometimes I think it's society which is disabled and not the handicapped person – it's society that rejects them, they don't reject society. And it's society's loss, because just like anyone else, a handicapped person can make a tremendous contribution.

We are luckier than most I think, in that Sarah isn't physically handicapped so she is mobile. She can't actually go anywhere without guidance but she can move – we are at present having a battle for mobility allowance for her. She's been turned down twice and will undoubtedly be turned down again – she can walk, you see – the fact that she can't go anywhere by herself in safety seems to be neither here nor there to the powers that be. I must say that we have found that we have had to fight to get any benefit. A Social Security lady told me (some years ago, mind) that there were no allowances for Sarah so I missed out on four years' attendance allowance. And the fight for mobility allowance continues. We are fortunate to have energy and ability to fight for Sarah's rights, but many people must be so exhausted with the effort of looking after a disabled person that they can't. It seems very wrong that one should have to fight so hard for what are supposed to be basic rights. Similarly the Health Services have given us until recently no support whatsoever. However, we have just recently been put in touch with a community nurse for the mentally handicapped who has offered us tremendous support and practical help, which has made a real difference. We are very lucky too in the sort of family support which we have, and that makes a real difference, but still the ultimate responsibility comes back to you, it's always there and can be very wearing. You worry about the future – what will happen to her when we can't look after her any more? We want to try and arrange some sort of sheltered community for her to live in, but places like that are few and far between, and would she be happy? I also wonder sometimes whether having a sister like Sarah affects her brothers. It must have some effect on them but I wonder if they get resentful. I know Liam does – at least he tells me that he gets sick of her at times. Mind you that's probably not abnormal at his age anyway (he's a year older than Sarah) and I do think it's good that he doesn't feel too inhibited or guilty about expressing how fed up he gets sometimes. I would hate to think he would feel responsible for Sarah and that he had to look after her when he was older. I think that would be wrong. Obviously I hope both boys will keep contact with her and see her and support her whatever happens, but I wouldn't like to think that their lives might be overshadowed by having to care for her.

That sounds really gloomy, but having Sarah isn't a gloomy thing – generally she is a great pleasure to have around and lovely to be with – if you can duck the odd right-hand jab! Undoubtedly though it does impose some restrictions on what you can do and what you can't do. For instance it is very difficult to take Sarah and Peter, who is three, out together unless there are two of us, as both children need a lot of attention. You can't get any shopping or anything for supervising the kids. Again, not a thing you think of generally, but a twelve-year-old would normally be a positive asset when looking after a toddler. I suppose it does make me feel a little sad sometimes when I see other girls of Sarah's age. What they can do and the sort of independence they can achieve, but really I'm not being sad for Sarah because most of the time she seems happy and content, and it's wrong to project our expectations on to others and to judge people by our standards for ourselves.

Parents of other handicapped kids are a great source of support and knowledge and it's very comforting to find that we all feel the same worries. One very frustrating aspect is the lack of information available to allow you to help yourself – I'm sure it's all available somewhere but finding it is another matter. I'm afraid the professionals don't seem to have any more success than we do in seeking out facts – and without facts we aren't really in a position to make any changes or improvements for ourselves or our relatives.

Our recent innovation is the organisation of a scheme to provide short-term relief to carers, by having the child go to another family for a day or so – up to twenty-four days a year. This has proved most beneficial to everyone – giving the rest of the family more freedom, and Sarah the opportunity to have a life of her own away from her immediate family. It is so nice for her to have a part of her social life which is totally her own, without us always there. It must drive her mad to always have us around too.

Sarah attends a Special School which we are very happy with, but we would like to see more real integration into the community for handicapped kids. Not that I can see that happening in the present economic climate. She also goes to a couple of youth clubs, which she enjoys very much. The idea of these was once again to try and give Sarah some independence. We ended up doing art with some of the kids at one club as they are short of helpers. It's great fun and we really enjoy it, but I must say sometimes we feel that a quiet night in would be nice. We wonder about Sarah as she gets older. It would be lovely to think perhaps she could meet someone and have an ordinary relationship with them – she couldn't have kids of course but I don't see why she should miss out on that aspect of relationships if she wants to have them. So many people have a strange idea about mentally handicapped people and sex. Don't know what they think they are going to do, but it certainly is a taboo subject. You think about what will happen in the future for your kids anyway, but more so for a handicapped child. They are always going to be your responsibility, emotionally if not practically – but I suppose all parents feel like that about their kids anyway. Perhaps it's more to do with being a parent than anything else. It will be strange when we don't have to look after Sarah any more. Not that she is any bother but it is knowing that she is there needing your attention. It sounds as if life caring for a handicapped child was full of gloom and doom and that's not true. It's generally just like looking after anyone – you do to a greater or lesser extent what needs to be done and hopefully get back a great deal in return. Yes it's hard work sometimes and sometimes you get fed up; but then one probably would anyway and also I feel that I am in a much more fortunate position than most because of the support I get. I could see it could be very difficult to cope without that sort of support, but I'm lucky and very thankful to have the help I have.

JIMMY DONALD

Jimmy lives in the North-East and had to give up a commercial career to care for his wife Kay, whose experience of developing multiple sclerosis was the subject of her contribution to RKP's *Images of Ourselves* edited by Jo Campling. They have three teenage sons.

I was born in Newcastle 56 years ago, my father was disabled and extremely self-conscious about his disability. I grew up on Tyneside in the 1930s in very poor circumstances as my father was never able to work.

After serving in the army towards the end of the war I returned to civvy street with no educational qualifications or any special skills. I had a number of jobs and managed to save to buy a house which my wife and I moved into after our honeymoon in 1956.

My wife had worked in a local store as a display artist until we were married. When our third child (the third boy) was born in 1964 my wife started to lose the feelings in her legs and could not do any of the numerous jobs she had been doing – running a house and looking after two small children and a baby.

Our GP arranged for my wife to see a neurologist at a local hospital. We had to wait quite some time before the appointment date; my wife didn't know what was wrong with her legs. She couldn't do any work and I had to give a lot of help with the children. It was a very trying time.

Her illness was diagnosed as multiple sclerosis (a disease of the central nervous system). It was shattering news to hear that there was no known cure for this disease and that my wife's condition would probably worsen through time. For months after her illness was diagnosed as I drove round on my job, I seemed to stop seeing people and could only see legs. Thousands of pairs of legs, running after buses, legs walking behind prams and pushchairs, legs getting on and off buses, legs going upstairs, legs going downstairs.

There seemed to be so many legs that were perfectly healthy, yet my wife's legs wouldn't function and probably NEVER would. It was something I couldn't shake off for a long time. It was now apparent that arrangements had to be made to keep the home going and to have the children looked after.

Not long before my wife took ill, I had changed jobs for the better or so I thought. It was a bad move as the firm were Dickensian in outlook and any salary increases meant going cap in hand to the boss. Normally I would have changed jobs, but no longer could I do what was best for me. Everything had to revolve round my wife and her inability to do her normal work. My wife was unable to get out of the house under her own steam so I was responsible for taking her to doctors, dentists, hospitals, etc. I was able to do this; one of the advantages of the job was that I didn't have to stay away from home for any length of time. So I reluctantly kept the same job as I was able to do things for my wife.

One of the first things that had to be done was arranging a rota of friends and relations to take out the baby; it wasn't an easy task, but eventually I managed to get a team of helpers who took him out regularly. They kept going for four years until he was old enough to get about by himself.

This was my first attempt at obtaining practical help. It wasn't easy – I was surprised at where the help came from and where it didn't come from. Looking after a disabled person and doing all the jobs that a disabled person is no longer able to do is a demanding job. In the early years of my wife's illness it was a very demanding job, particularly as we had three children to look after.

The local Social Services provided a home help to do some of the housework. She came each morning but there was so much for me to do each evening when I returned from work. Apart from the strain placed on me by all the work, there was the financial strain. The job I was in was selling. Normally a salesman is paid on results (commission). My firm thought commission was a dirty word and in spite of personally achieving good results and in spite of the firm making a considerable amount of money, I still received a pittance. So much so that I had to apply to the local authority along with the unemployed to receive vouchers for free school uniforms, free shoes and free school meals for the children. I found this humiliating as I wasn't unemployed. I worked very hard and could never really escape from the job as my phone never seemed to stop ringing in the evening.

The years that should have been the happiest in a marriage when the children were small were very hard going. This period was one where I felt the whole family missed out. My wife was unable to go out with the children, take them to the seaside or the country, etc. I had to keep going in my job and try to give the children the care and attention they normally would have received. Looking after them as well as doing a job plus the thousand and one things that had to be done round the house, was just an added responsibility instead of it being a pleasure. The house we had moved into when we first married was now physically unsuitable. It was a three-storey house and my wife could no longer climb stairs. She was now confined to a wheelchair. We eventually found a house that lent itself to disabled living.

About the time my wife took ill I had just completed a course in local history and qualified as a tour guide with a voluntary group of history enthusiasts. Unfortunately I was unable to play a full role in this organisation as caring for my wife was taking more and more of my time.

Caring drains you physically and mentally. Physically when you are attending to the disabled person and mentally in that you leave the person for any length of time, you are always wondering, will she be all right? Has she fallen from her wheelchair? You can never 'switch off'.

I've been a carer for almost twenty years now. The load does not get any lighter. In those years I've conditioned myself to just living and working for a disabled person.

The disabled person usually leans very heavily on the carer, with no let up as the carer gets older. Whenever I go out for the shortest time, my wife wants to know when I will be back. The business of always saying where you are going and when you will be back has gone to ridiculous extremes as I find myself telling my wife when I am going into another room or when I am going to the bathroom. A carer cannot be ill but must keep going every day of the year. You dread catching a cold or getting flu because you just cannot retire to bed for a few days.

Some years ago I hurt my back rather badly and I suffer frequently from pain. Pushing a wheelchair does not help. On one occasion I had a really bad do with my back and could hardly walk because of excruciating pain. On top of that, I caught flu. I was sitting wrapped in a blanket in front of the TV twisting and turning, trying to ease the back pain and feeling pretty rotten, when my wife came into the room and said 'Don't forget it's your day to do the dishes.' It was just another day.

Caring for a disabled person means that you spend far more time in each other's company than would happen with an able-bodied couple. This puts a great strain on the relationship. A lot of people cannot accept the situation and marriages in which one of the partners contracts multiple sclerosis often break up, usually with the husband leaving a disabled wife. When a husband contracts multiple sclerosis the wife usually sticks by him. Women seem to have more 'guts' than men.

I have never regretted my marriage for a moment in spite of the circumstances and I am sure that if I had ended up in a wheelchair my wife would have stuck by me. Some three years ago I was made redundant. What a relief it was to get rid of that job. This gave me a breathing space – a chance to assess my situation. My wife was needing more and more care. She was leaning on me very heavily and I decided that it wouldn't be practical to take on another full-time job. My time is now taken up mainly with looking after my wife, doing shopping, housework, etc. I try to take my wife out as much as possible, but we are restricted to going to places that have suitable disabled persons' toilets.

We can't just go anywhere unless we know the facilities are right. I usually go beforehand to check that a place is suitable for us to visit.

After I was made redundant I was able to take up my local history interests. I find this completely relaxes me and it is a complete contrast to the mental load the caring places on me. We are both on the committee of the local branch of the Multiple Sclerosis Society and getting involved in this way helps me to see further than my own problems, and makes me realise that I'm not the only carer around.

We live simply on pensions my wife receives and a pension I receive for looking after her. I've no complaint about local Social Services, they have helped by providing a ground-floor bathroom for my wife and a fitted kitchen designed around her disability.

We haven't had a holiday in years, although the money for one could possibly be found, my wife would like a holiday and she would like it to be with me. I think I'm reluctant to go on holiday with her because it wouldn't be a holiday for me. I would still be the carer, still always 'switched on'.

We lead a limited social life. So many places are inaccessible or don't have suitable toilets and an evening out means so much preparation beforehand that I often feel I'd rather not go out. My wife gets a great deal of pleasure from TV and is reluctant to go out on any evening when one of her favourite programmes is showing.

Only one son is at home now, although the other two live nearby and I can get out if I know that one of them will be in the house during my absence.

My wife's memory is now very poor and she has lost the ability to make decisions of any kind. This adds to the strain as I find I am having to do the remembering and deciding for two people not just myself. When a carer is seen to be looking after a disabled person people often say 'You are doing a wonderful job' and then pass on to get on with their own particular thing. You are left very much to get on by yourself.

What the future holds I can't imagine. We just seem to live life a day at a time. I try to keep reasonably fit so that I will always be able to look after my wife, but no matter how much you wish to take care of a loved one, there is a physical limit to the amount you can do. If I was unable to look after my wife, there is only one long-term care establishment where she could go in this town and that is a Victorian hospital that local disabled people try to avoid at all costs. So I must keep going.

I sometimes think what might happen if I was ever relieved of the task of caring for my wife and one thing always keeps springing to mind – I might get rid of the pain in my back!

CHRISTINE DARBY

Christine's husband has multiple sclerosis and they live with their two teenage sons in Essex. Christine has a particular interest in carers' physical health problems and has compiled a guide to keep fit for caring.

'No, No, No, No,' I kept screaming. I couldn't hear what else the specialist said because after 'Your husband's case is a tragic one, he has multiple sclerosis', the continuous screaming went on and on inside my head. I appeared quite calm and even experienced that freezing of emotion you get at first when someone dear to you dies, but at the core of me that screaming didn't stop for weeks. It didn't stop in fact until I had persuaded our doctor that George should be told he had multiple sclerosis. I pointed out that we had promised never to have secrets from each other and that he would never forgive me for knowing the nature of his illness but not telling him what it was, while he struggled through the library medical books progressing from leukaemia to brain tumours. It seemed to me that if he was going to become totally dependent on me then that dependence would have to be built on trust, or our enforced binding together would be purgatory. Once George and I could discuss his illness his matter-of-fact attitude helped me. He was not at all dramatic about it, just took a practical approach, pointing out that at least we had time to prepare for his possible disablement even while harbouring our hope that the multiple sclerosis would not strike again. By chance we had just moved to a house with a downstairs bathroom, but there was a bit of decorating and cupboard building we wanted done, so as soon as George's 'legs came back' we got on with it. We also did as many of those energetic things we had planned to do 'one day' whenever the opportunity presented itself to try and avoid later regrets of 'if only we had done that when we could'. We also started our family as soon as fate decreed we could! I had been plagued since my teens with back trouble caused by a torn back muscle and, although I hoped I wouldn't need to do any heavy nursing, I found an understanding physiotherapist and every day from then on I did a few minutes' back exercise. My back trouble cleared up, so it benefited me as well as enabling me to do the heavy lifting when the need arose – but I didn't actually perform these exercises when George was around, as I thought it would seem to be rather a gloomy attitude for me to be taking at that time!

We had been married only a year when we found George had multiple sclerosis. It was quite sudden. One morning George simply found he could not get out of bed! The first emotional effect it had on us was to make us grow up rather fast and this made us oddly lonely to begin with, as we began to feel wiser than our friends and longed to be able to teach them what we now knew (serious illness is a great sorter-out of priorities) and help them to stop worrying about trivialities. We learned suddenly how to live each day for itself and enjoy it and savour it. We appreciated young healthy life in a way unusual for young people who tend to take these things for granted. This special wisdom which at that time distanced us so slightly from our friends, brought us much closer to each other and also brought us the unexpected pleasure of the friendship of much older people.

The use of George's legs came back after the first multiple sclerosis attack, but he lost the use of them again quite suddenly when our elder boy was nineteen months old and the younger two months. The next few months were the hardest I had to cope with. If George was to keep his job I had to drive him to work until we could get hand controls fitted to the car. So I had to learn to drive quickly – something I should have faced before, but had foolishly put off because I hated driving. At this time I felt very isolated. George hated being suddenly so dependent on me just at a time when he wanted to help me. His very thoughtfulness for my welfare made his suffering worse. We had to get up early and cope with the new routine of getting George dressed and washed, etc. when newly 'legless'. We had the young children to get up, too, then I had to drive George to work and clear up, shop, wash nappies, etc. and be ready to drive to collect him and bring him back from work. Friends would have helped but there was so little time to see them and I was so continually and desperately tired.

I found it very hard (and still do!) to watch George struggling to do something for himself when I could easily do it for him, but I do not want him to feel later that I forcibly took his independence from him. His increasing dependence has to be 'voluntary', so to speak. Sometimes, however, my own emotional needs demand that I take action if I am to avoid feeling martyred. For instance, it took quite some time for us both to acknowledge after the birth of our second child that George was not going to recover the use of his legs. He could drag himself just a few yards using his walking frame and he kept this up for ages, just around the house and office, but never able to go out elsewhere. We then had the most miserable holiday of our lives with me stuck interminably with toddler and baby, forever tramping about with the pram, or on the beach or in a playground, while George sat in the hotel. It took me sometime to approach George about the use of a wheelchair so that we could do things together again. We both felt a certain amount of psychological resistance to the wheelchair idea and tried hiring one first, on a 'temporary' basis. The children overcame any great tragic intensity we might have given to the first wheelchair excursion by immediately climbing on to George's lap and sitting there wild with excitement and yelling delightedly 'Mind the pram! Mind the pram!' all the way down the road.

The tiredness associated with looking after someone disabled was the hardest thing for me to adjust to. I gave up doing all housework which was not essential and then gave up things I had previously thought were essential and now decided were not! I do not think anyone can ever understand the perpetual tiredness of a carer unless they have experienced it for themselves. The tiredness is, of course, due to different causes for each carer, but the exhaustive effect is the same – for me the tiredness comes from the physical exertion of caring for someone with severe multiple sclerosis and from the mental stress of seeing the person you love best in the world suffering from such a disease. At first the disabled person does not seem to appreciate the exhaustion of the carer – probably because the carer is so set on keeping up the dependant's morale that they make light of the effect which that dependence is having on them. This often seems to be exacerbated by the initial tendency of the wheelchair-bound to continue to offer help and get involved in outside affairs as they did when independent, not realising that such offers can no longer be carried through by themselves but involve more work for the carer. This situation is made even worse by the fact that you are now in contact through hospitals, etc. with an unlimited supply of similar 'victims' so many of whom are much worse off than yourself and you long to help. It is hard for the carer to get over to the wheelchair-bound person that there is now a physical limit on them both and on the help they can now offer to others, without the feeling that their reluctance to help appears merely churlish and dog-in-the manger. If you go on about having your hands full enough already, you make your dependant feel a burden to you, and if you don't explain, then you sound as if you are being mean and unco-operative!

Never, in any crisis, has the welfare state as such been of any practical use. Doctors can do very little to relieve any relapse George experiences, he just has to come through it and we wait to see what movement will come back after an attack of multiple sclerosis. While ill he is often quite helpless, only able to move his head. I have never been offered a night nurse to help while he has been ill. Twice I have urgently requested (after a particularly heavy night's work) the help of a district nurse just for the early morning toileting (we do not need to have a regular visit) and on each occasion I have been refused the help as the nurse was 'too busy'. The Social Services in our area have never been of help after the initial burst of assistance with walking frame and wheelchair. Their lack of help seems to be through ignorance rather than ill-will! We are lucky to have neighbours and friends who are very supportive, but of course, no one can be expected to do more than relieve you of the physical exertion for a couple of hours during the day until you can regain the energy to carry on. I have been enormously helped, however, by friends who have just quietly slipped in and taken my washing to do, or who have rolled up and cleaned the house through and done the shopping. We have also had help from a local access group run on a voluntary basis by an incredible lady, Audrey Fowles, from her wheelchair. She is a fount of information and wisdom and also of moral support – would that the Social Services took a few lessons from her!

Mrs A. was dominated by her mother in childhood and adult life and had to elope in order to marry when she was 37 years old. Two years later her husband died and mother once again asserted a great emotional hold. Mrs A. now has leukaemia.

ELIZABETH REID

With four elderly dependants and a five-year-old son, Elizabeth has somehow managed to find time to go to evening classes and to promote the work of the Association of Carers. She and her family live in Kilmarnock, Scotland.

My voyage into caring started with me being the invalid. In December 1979 I was taken ill with glandular fever. This had been caused partially because I was so run down because of running my own home and also seeing to the needs of my own parents and parents-in-law, all of whom had debilitating diseases.

Father had chronic bronchitis and by this time only part of a stomach, a lengthy operation in 1968 had left him in great pain and any food or medication did little to help.

Mother had angina and low blood pressure all aggravated by the fact my father at this point had been mostly confined to bed for four years.

Father-in-Law had Parkinson's disease – this gives rise to incontinence and causes depression and irritability.

Mother-in-Law in a wheelchair because of arthritis – she also has co-ordination problems, speech problems, a stomach ulcer and a hiatus hernia.

Anyhow back to my story in 1979. My parents came to try and look after me and also my son who was then less than 2 years old. He was an active, intelligent child who needed constant amusing and did not need much sleep; it was rare for him to sleep all night. In June 1980 my parents' doctor said it was inadvisable for my parents to go home because my mother by this time was not fit to look after herself at home and my father was mostly confined to bed. So we sold our semi-detached villa-type home for a bungalow so my parents would have no stairs to climb for bathrooms, etc. I was still far from well but at least we were managing. The district nurse had started coming in and we now paid for a home help for a few hours a week.

Note

(1) DHSS will not give money to pay for home help if invalid is a blood relative.
(2) Council will not provide one if husband is working.

My parents-in-law were deteriorating. My mother-in-law was virtually housebound and my father-in-law was finding shopping and paying bills, etc. too difficult. Because of the effect of Parkinson's disease on the memory he frequently lost stamps, money, etc. When they were no longer able to come to me for meals at weekends I used to leave a meal for the ones at home then put food and myself into a taxi and go to them (they had meals on wheels during the week – well at least my father-in-law did – my mother-in-law refused them, by this time she was very ill with persistent diarrhoea because of lack of proper feeding and hygiene problems). The district nurse and doctors were there sometimes twice or three times a week. The crunch came on Christmas Eve, 1980, when I had to have an ambulance deliver them to me. Christmas was a nightmare. Both my parents were in bed ill, also now my mother-in-law. That meant Christmas dinner for seven, three of which had to be served in bed. My son at this point was only 2½, and my husband worked unsocial hours. The strain on our marriage was horrendous. It took until Boxing Day to get my mother-in-law into hospital. There she stayed for six weeks. During this time my father-in-law remained with us. It had now become abundantly clear to me that my parents-in-law could not manage on their own. My husband and sister-in-law, however, did not agree with me. So all hell broke loose.

In mid-February 1981 my mother-in-law was discharged from hospital. Within two weeks the doctor had sent round the health visitor to say either I took them or they went into long-term care. In our part of the country that meant separating them. There were no units equipped to cope with couples who needed so much attention. What a dilemma – how could I take my own parents and push my parents-in-law into a hospital for perhaps the next ten years? The decision had to be taken by me. My husband wanted no part of it, nor did my sister-in-law. She was 600 miles away with a secure job, no family, so there was no help from anyone. My own health was still far from good. Anyhow despite the odds I felt it was the right thing to do to take everyone. Call it faith in God or just pure cussedness, anyhow I went ahead. At this time my husband won a trip to America because of his outstanding sales achievement so off we went and had a marvellous time. The problems would wait and so they did. On 28 February I bought a huge Victorian house. Its last owner had been an old man of 80. It had not been modernised for years – you name it and it needed fixing!

The cost was horrendous. There was no financial help from any of our dependants. They had always been in council houses so it was a matter of getting them cleared out and that was that. We invested every penny in 6 London Road and borrowed to the hilt to do the repairs. Two and a half years later we are still sorting and borrowing. We built a downstairs shower room for my parents-in-law – 90 per cent grants were advertised for the disabled.

We were foiled again, because the house belonged to my husband and so only a 50 per cent grant. The DHSS were supposed to make up the difference, but 2½ years later I am still waiting. There were initially many problems caring for so many people with their varying needs and temperaments. After all I was a wife, a mother, a daughter and a daughter-in-law all at the same time. Meal times were a major headache when we moved to London Road with everyone. My son Michael had just turned three. Sometimes both my father and father-in-law were so ill they had to be spoon fed, a very tiring process without having six other people to feed as well. In July 1981 my health broke again and I was sent to hospital for a week. All the social workers, doctors, everyone who was supposed to know best said, 'I told you so, you should not have taken everyone.' I wept often, through a combination of frustration, and weakness, but the feeling still persisted that I was doing 'God's will', my mission in life if you like. Money was very tight. My parents were very generous (unhappily not so my in-laws). I could not get the DHSS to give me control over pensions, allowances, etc. Some old people are under the impression they can be kept for nothing and that their pensions, etc. are for putting in the bank. This was the case with my father-in-law. The situation did not alter until December 1981 when he was taken to hospital and was no longer fit to dictate, since then I have had control and give him back £14.00 per week. He also has a private pension. In October 1981 my own father died at home; he had been with me nearly two years and had been in and out of hospital in that time. I loved him dearly and miss him still. There are tears in my eyes as I write this. We had a wonderful relationship and he caused no waves or disruptions.

He suffered much pain, and my belief in God and a better hereafter is a comfort to me in my loss. After my father's death, money was very tight. We had lost a pension and partial attendance allowance. My husband put the house on the market with no thought of its occupants. My mother was in bed nearly constantly for six months after my father died. Also around the beginning of December 1981 my father-in-law was taken so ill he had to be hospitalised for six weeks. This was when I gained more financial control and was consequently able to pay bills and take the house off the market.

My next crisis came in February 1982, when my mother had been more or less confined to bed since my father's death in October 1981. My father-in-law was released from hospital in January 1982. Although still not well, it was a dreadful cold winter, and everyone was at a very low ebb. Then I took ill again. My parents-in-law were taken into care and my mother was in hospital. Happily spring arrived, and my mother came home from hospital a lot better. My parents-in-law returned from care, more grateful for their 'comforts of home'. The next chaos was when my mother-in-law had a bad fall in the toilet, and had to be taken to hospital, because she had injured her spine. This was in May 1982. She had to spend about three weeks in bed. Around this time as well, my father-in-law had gone blind in one eye so I also had to take him to eye clinics. Not only had he now got Parkinson's disease, he was now only partially sighted, sometimes totally blind, but these turns come and go. Around this time, provisions were made for my father-in-law to go to a day hospital. This relieved his boredom and irritability. Unfortunately at this point in time my mother-in-law, because of her fall, could no longer walk and wheelchairs were banned from the day hospital (stupid but true!). However, one intensive course of physiotherapy – both at home and at hospital – got her mobile enough to meet their requirements (only just, but they now take her). This also gives her a bath – a luxury she had not experienced for a long time. It had, by February 1982, become too dangerous to allow her in the shower even with myself and the district nurse in attendance, her mobility had decreased so she could only be bed-bathed. This sort of brings things up to the present day.

My mother is in much better health at present. Her depression, which she suffered after my father's death, is lifting. She is a great help with Michael who is now five and ready for school.

My parents-in-law now go two days a week to the day hospital and every six months they are taken into hospital to give me two weeks' break.

Weekends are non-existent. There is only emergency cover. There is no bedding down service in our area, so nights out are rare. My last night out was when a friend came in from the Red Cross and put my mother-in-law to bed. Family help is non-existent. I am an only daughter and my sister-in-law lives in the south of England. Cash help is at a premium; the form filling, delay and incompetence of the DHSS is untrue.

The amount of dangerous drugs I hand out is frightening, I

have enough stuff here to overdose the whole street. I have advertised for unpaid help to take my mother-in-law out in her wheelchair – no takers! Everything has to run like clockwork. I always have to have enough medication, food, etc. in case anyone gets worse and I am unable to leave the house. This situation, however, is not so chronic now. I have also acquired an uncle who stays with us. He has had problems with marriage and health, but compared to the rest is very fit, so he helps with the garden, shopping and walking the dog which is great. I try to grow some vegetables; it does help the money situation when one has seven mouths to feed.

Would I do it again? I hear you ask. Yes, I think so. It has given me a great insight into life, death and suffering. It is, however, a heavy cross to bear. Not always easy to change wet beds and empty commodes if you do not feel 100 per cent yourself, bearing in mind my mother-in-law is 13 stone, I am 6 stone.

With the cut-backs in services I can see a future when families will need to take more care of their parents. Not a pleasant thought – I can see it from both sides. I do not think I would like to be as dependent on my daughter-in-law as my mother-in-law is on me. All the personal intimate things which I have to do are very humbling to both patient and carer.

Other points

Aids I have in the home

2 Wheelchairs – One normal for indoors; one battery for outdoors
1 Zimmer
1 Toilet seat and rail
1 Bath seat
1 Houkey pull
2 Commodes
Incontinence pads and paper sheets

It has taken me nearly six months to get a supply of paper sheets. I was told 'No' by the doctor's receptionist, health visitor, community care office. I received them this morning by ambulance *stolen* by caring staff who understand how much mess is caused when someone with Parkinson's disease needs an enema and is too weak after it to even get up to a commode. The mess, the smell and the time involved is unreal.

Doctors

On the whole very helpful but get fed-up when there is nothing else they can do. You feel as though you are always on the phone for something or other. The day my father died I phoned for a doctor around 2 p.m. 2nd October. No one came. I phoned emergency at around 8 p.m. This doctor did come at 1.30 a.m. 3rd October, when my father died. I think the first phone call was disregarded because the doctor did not believe me my father's condition was so bad. I do not blame them there is only so much a human being can do.

Health visitors

Very nice but ineffectual – their hands are tied by lack of finance, lack of resources, and loyalty to the doctors they serve.

District nurses

Very understaffed, overworked band of ladies who are only in about 15 minutes twice a week so cannot really appreciate the problems seven days a week, 24 hours a day.

Day hospitals

Are a great idea from the carers' point of view, it gives them a few hours to please themselves. However, getting up before 7 a.m. to get two people washed, dressed and breakfast for 9 o'clock for the ambulance coming, one wonders sometimes if it is worth it.

Two-week hospital stays
This is also very nice from the carer's view point. The problems the week before are dreadful. You get all sorts of tantrums. I think my parents-in-law are afraid sometimes I won't have them back. The temptation is very great. The freedom one has from routine is tremendous. My son can make as much noise as he likes.

Smells
Unless one is used to working with invalids one does not realise sick, old people smell. No amount of clean clothes, bed clothes, air fresheners, disinfectants can help. The decaying smell lingers especially if incontinence is a problem.

Myself
My own life has been enhanced by my trials. I am self-assured and must appear to many as bossy and domineering. This attitude I think is necessary. It is my home, it would be easy to slip into the role of 'wee girl' and be subservient to my elders, this I think is a great trap. However, as my husband pointed out, they need me more than I need them. *Hard but true.*

Space and privacy
I am lucky with this house. I have a large lounge, dining room, 5 bedrooms, 3 bathrooms. Everyone can spread out. The large lounge is used mostly by everyone during the day. Meals are generally taken as a family, although we do not all eat at the same time. After tea my parents-in-law watch TV in the dining room. The lounge then becomes the province of my husband, son, myself. My mother has a comfortable large bed-sit with colour TV, so everyone is well provided for.

I have 6 TV sets so everyone is catered for whether they are up or confined to bed. One night last winter everything went bang. On checking I discovered I was burning, 4 TV sets, 5 electric blankets, 2 fires, 1 kettle and about 10 lights. Luckily the fault was outside and nothing to do with my load. The bills as you can imagine are horrendous.

How do I see my life in years to come? Well I would like to achieve 5 'O'-levels and two highers. One of my geriatricians suggested after that I do a Social Science course, she says then when she needs a social worker who really knows her onions, she will employ me. That, however, could be years away. I am not God, I don't have a master plan. I just go from day to day and pray.

Since I started writing this my mother has been bedridden because of the severity of heart pains and low blood pressure. These attacks can last weeks, days or months. It is three years since her own GP said she was unable to cope with life on her own. Despite applications and appeals the DHSS in their wisdom do not see her as a person who should receive even a partial attendance allowance.

Well I think this about covers everything.

JOAN CLARK

Joan had to leave a professional job in education when she was in her fifties to care for Dorothy, her sister, an ex-teacher suffering from multiple sclerosis, and her mother, who had a series of strokes. As a single woman she did manage to qualify for Invalid Care Allowance but lost it on her sixtieth birthday. She is now trying to rebuild her own life in her native North-East of England.

When Joan's sister Dorothy developed multiple sclerosis she was forced to retire from teaching. Joan gave up her own career in education to move to lower-paid jobs nearer home. Finally she was forced to give up paid work altogether and forfeited pay and pension rights. Fortunately, Dorothy had been teaching long enough for her to have a good invalidity pension in her own right. After a few years their mother had a stroke and Joan spent some years caring for both – mother's will to stay alive while

Dorothy still lived seemed immense. For some time Joan claimed attendance allowance for only one of her relatives as she didn't think it was 'right' she should claim two. After some procrastination by the local DHSS she eventually got invalid care allowance, as a single woman, but lost it when she reached 60, pensionable age. She agreed to keep the following diary for a week.

A week in the life of. . . .

Thursday

12.15 a.m.	Mother awake . . . given warm drink.
3.15 a.m.	Dorothy called . . . wet . . . washed, creamed, clean pad . . . turned.
7.15 a.m.	Dorothy called . . .wanted to spend penny . . . put on commode. After half an hour had not passed water . . . Gave her her breakfast. Had bath myself and dressed. Put Dorothy back to bed. Had my own breakfast.
9.00 a.m.	Helped bathing service lift, bath and dress mother. Gave mother her breakfast. Washed breakfast dishes. Spoke to neighbour for a few minutes.
10.15 a.m.	Helped nurse to lift Dorothy, bath her and wash her hair. Set Dorothy's hair. Removed superfluous hair from her chin. Made beds . . . made coffee. Prepared and cooked pizza for lunch. Prepared salad, etc., for tea for mother and sitter.
12.00 noon	Lunch. (Entailed cutting up food small, helping both to feed, constantly wiping dribbles, etc.)
12.30 p.m.	Mother to rest. Dorothy to rest. Washed coffee and lunch dishes. Ironed few things.
2.30 p.m.	Got mother up. Sitter came. I went to get prescriptions. Returned – got Dorothy up,

	washed and changed her. Tidied beds. Washed and changed myself.
4.00 p.m.	Dorothy and I went out for tea.
8.15 p.m.	Returned home. Sitter went home. Drink and biscuit for M and D.
9.00 p.m.	Nurse came and we put M and D to bed.
9.40 p.m.	Nurse left. I tidied up where necessary and set breakfast trays.
10.00 p.m.	Watched news on T.V. Glanced at paper, wrote diary. Got undressed.
11.45 p.m.	Looked at Mother. Turned Dorothy and gave her sleeping pill.
12.00 midnight	Bed. Read for a while.

Friday

6.30 a.m.	Looked at Mother. Turned Dorothy.
8.45 a.m.	Bath and dressed.
9.15 a.m.	Gave Mother and Dorothy breakfast. Both needed help. Had own breakfast. Put washing in. Inspected 'cabbage patch'. Pulled out a few weeds. Parcelled newspapers and put out with rubbish. Mother tired so lay down again and went to sleep.
10.00 a.m.	Dealt with business letter. Phoned to thank friends we visited on Thursday. Wrote shopping list for afternoon. Got pension books signed by M and D. Sat and talked with each of them for a while (both almost unable to speak in return). Hung washing out. Helped nurse wash and dress Dorothy.
11.00 a.m.	Made beds. Prepared lunch and put on to cook. Took Dorothy for a walk (in chair).
12.00 noon	Dorothy and I had lunch – stew, yoghurt, coffee.
12.45 p.m.	Put Dorothy to bed for a rest. Got Mother up. Washed and dressed her and gave her lunch. Made bed. Prepared tea.

2.00 p.m.	Got Dorothy up.
2.15 p.m.	Sitter came and I went for pensions and shopping for self and neighbour.
4.30 p.m.	Returned home. Had tea together.
5.45 p.m.	Sitter went home. Washed dishes, brought washing in, cut Mother's and Dorothy's nails.
6.15 p.m.	Visitor.
7.00 p.m.	Watched 'Gardener's World'.
7.30 p.m.	Prepared supper for Dorothy and Mother. Cheese omelette and coffee. Both needed help with eating and drinking.
8.00 p.m.	Vacuumed and dusted bedrooms. Read bits of paper to M and D.
9.00 p.m.	Helped nurse put M and D to bed.
9.30 p.m.	Had my own supper, washed dishes, set breakfast trays.
10.00 p.m.	Dorothy coughing. Helped her to get phlegm up. Did some mending, wrote letter, wrote diary.
11.30 p.m.	Looked at M and D and gave her sleeping pill. Bed.

Saturday

6.00 p.m.	Dorothy called . . . wet . . . washed, creamed, changed, turned. Looked at Mother. I woke with a slight migraine. Took Alka Seltzer.
8.30 a.m.	Very sick. Took another Alka Seltzer. Bathed, dressed.
9.15 a.m.	Helped nurse with Dorothy.
9.40 a.m.	Gave Dorothy breakfast, gave Mother breakfast, both needed help. Mother tired . . . stayed in bed. Made other beds.
10.30 a.m.	Vac'ed and dusted Dorothy's room, sitting room, hall. Put meat in and prepared vegetables.
11.15 a.m.	Coffee, washed dishes, talked with Dorothy till dinner time.

12.30 p.m.	Dinner . . . lamb, sponge roll, coffee.
1.15 p.m.	Dorothy to rest. Feel better myself now. Mother got up, washed, given dinner.
2.00 p.m.	Went to shops to collect bread and prescriptions. Returned, washed dishes, made M's bed. Made cake and scones, defrosted fridge.
3.30 p.m.	Visitor for twenty minutes. Dorothy up. Tidied bed.
4.30 p.m.	Tea. Washed dishes, cleared away Friday's washing. Half an hour in the garden.
7.00 p.m.	Read paper to Mother and Dorothy.
7.30 p.m.	Went to water friend's plants.
8.00 p.m.	Got supper ready (bacon and egg).
8.15 p.m.	Watched 'Val Doonican Show'.
9.00 p.m.	Helped nurse put Mother and Dorothy to bed. Washed dishes, set breakfast trays, watered plants, tidied up, wrote diary, wrote 'Get Well' note.
11.00 p.m.	Got undressed, turned Dorothy and gave her sleeping pill. Early to bed.

Sunday

3.45 a.m.	Called by Dorothy . . . wet . . . washed, creamed, changed, turned. Mother awake . . . given warm drink.
8.30 a.m.	Got up . . . bathed, dressed. Stuffed chicken, prepared vegetables.
9.15 a.m.	Washed Dorothy's lower half and picked her up. Made breakfast, gave Dorothy her breakfast . . . she needed help. Helped Mother with her breakfast, settled her down for more sleep. Had own breakfast, washed dishes.
10.45 a.m.	Nurse washed and dressed Dorothy. Coffee, put chicken in to cook, made beds. Watched part of Service on television (and 'Link').
12.00 noon	Dorothy and I had dinner. Chicken, ice cream, coffee.

1.00 p.m.	Dorothy to rest, got Mother up, washed, dressed, given dinner, made her bed. Washed dishes, prepared tea.
2.15 p.m.	Sitter came. Got Dorothy up, went to Ashington to see Aunt.
4.45 p.m.	Returned . . . Dorothy tired, put to rest. Planted some beans and cabbages. Washed tea dishes. Read paper to Mother, till Dorothy called. Felt her bowels were going to move. On commode for half an hour. Nothing happened, so I put her back on bed and helped movement to start (it is often necessary to do this). Got her up again.
6.40 p.m.	Watched some of 'Hymns of Praise' and Election Broadcast. Made supper . . . salad, cold chicken, coffee. Had supper and watched some of 'Eurogala'.
8.45 p.m.	Helped nurse to put Mother and Dorothy to bed.
9.30 p.m.	Washed dishes, set breakfast trays, tidied up as needed. Put washing in, made posy to take to hospital in the morning, watered plants I had planted earlier, put milk bottles out. Wrote diary. Got ready for bed. Glanced at paper.
11.15 p.m.	Dorothy called . . . wet . . . washed, creamed, changed, turned, pill. Looked at Mother.
11.45 p.m.	Bed. Read a while.

Monday

4.00 a.m.	Dorothy called. Turned.
8.30 a.m.	I bathed, dressed and had breakfast.
9.30 a.m.	Washed Dorothy's lower half. Lifted her up and helped her with her breakfast. Gave Mother her breakfast in bed.
10.00 a.m.	Friend came and stayed while I went to hospital with flowers.

10.30 a.m.	Nurse came (stranger) so I had to show her where the things were and she finished washing Dorothy and dressed her. Coffee with visitor.
11.15 a.m.	Put dinner on . . . boiled bacon, onions, carrots. Visitor left. Made beds. Tidied Dorothy's bedroom and put dry washing away.
11.45 a.m.	Neighbour came in for a few minutes.
12.30 a.m.	Dorothy and I had dinner . . . as above, plus yoghurt.
1.30 p.m.	Dorothy to rest, washed dishes (rare pile!).
2.00 p.m.	Got mother up, washed, dressed, given dinner, changed her bed. Started to give garage a good 'do'.
3.30 p.m.	Dorothy ready to get up, very wet, washed, creamed, changed clothes.
4.00 p.m.	Tea. Finished garage, swept front, took up a few weeds, put washing in. Read paper to M and D.
6.30 p.m.	Watched part of 'Crossroads' and 'Ask the Family'.
7.30 p.m.	Took Dorothy for a walk in chair.
8.00 p.m.	Supper . . . fish baked with savory rice.
9.00 p.m.	Nurse came in and we put M and D to bed (Mother not very well. Very heavy to move and lift).
9.45 p.m.	Washed dishes, set breakfast trays, washed kitchen floor. Read *Evening Chronicle* for a while. Mother and Dorothy's postal votes dealt with. Spent half an hour getting Dorothy's throat clear, turned, pill.
11.00 p.m.	Wrote diary, got ready for bed, looked at Mother.
12.00 midnight	To bed with *Hitler's Eva*.

Tuesday (moved to bungalow a year ago today)

3.15 a.m.	Turned Dorothy and looked at Mother.

9.00 a.m.	Bathed and dressed, made breakfast, lifted Dorothy up and helped her with her breakfast, hung washing out.
10.00 a.m.	Nurse came to bath Dorothy and wash hair and help me with Mother.
11.00 a.m.	Coffee. Washed dishes, made beds, changed Dorothy's and my bed.
12.30 p.m.	Lunch . . . soup, cold boiled bacon, salad, coffee, biscuit.
1.30 p.m.	Dorothy to bed. Washed dishes, put Mother in front doorway while I worked in garden – nice and sunny.
3.45 p.m.	Dorothy got up. I went to corner shop for some bread.
4.30 p.m.	Tea . . . savoury sausage pie.
5.30 p.m.	Dorothy had further rest as we were going out later. Washed dishes, brought in washing, ironed, made coffee, etc., for sitter.
6.30 p.m.	Dorothy up, washed, changed, ready to go out.
7.00 p.m.	Nurse came (by arrangement) to help me put Mother to bed as she was up early. Sitter (friend) came.
7.20 p.m.	I took D to friends' in chair.
10.00 p.m.	Returned home. Sitter went away. I put D to bed with sleeping pill. Mother wakened . . . wet, changed, washed, given warm drink.
11.00 p.m.	Wrote diary, washed dishes, set breakfast trays. Dorothy having trouble with throat again tonight. Helped to relieve situation.
12.00 midnight	Got ready for bed. Had milky drink, and went to bed with book as usual.

Wednesday

5.30 a.m.	Dorothy called . . . wet . . . changed, washed, creamed, turned.
8.45 a.m.	I got up, bathed, dressed, made my bed, made

	breakfast. Washed D's lower half and picked her up again for breakfast. Sat beside her to help her and had my own at the same time.
10.00 a.m.	Nurse came, finished washing and dressing Dorothy. Home help comes on Wednesdays – 10.00 a.m. to 1.00 p.m. Washed dishes, made Dorothy's bed, put meat to cook, prepared vegetables.
11.30 a.m.	Mother much better today. Got her up, washed, dressed; coffee. Went to deliver a message while home help was here.
12.15 p.m.	Put veg's on, and dumplings in stew, prepared supper.
1.00 p.m.	Took help home.
1.15 p.m.	Dinner.
2.00 p.m.	Dorothy to rest. Washed dishes, prepared tea, tried to rouse Mother's interest in something, anything, not much luck.
3.45 p.m.	Got Dorothy up, wet, washed, changed.
4.15 p.m.	Tea. Half an hour in garden, took washing in, cleaned car. Took Dorothy for a walk, in chair.
7.30 p.m.	Supper . . . kilted sausages cooked with savoury rice.
8.00 p.m.	Sir Robert Mayer concert on T.V. Did some mending.
9.00 p.m.	Helped nurse put M and D to bed. Washed dishes, set breakfast trays, ironed, glanced at paper.
11.15 p.m.	Got ready for bed, turned Dorothy, pill. Wrote letter and diary, looked at Mother.
12.00 midnight	Bed with book.

Thursday. . . .

MARGARET PARKINSON

Margaret was a very early member of the Association of Carers and acts as its contact for the Rochester area. Her husband, a double amputee, supports her in this.

Retired at 54! It seemed impossible when my husband broke the news that he was to be medically retired. He was suffering from emphysema, which was getting a great deal worse with the dust in the office where he worked. With two daughters still at school, it seemed a daunting prospect. It turned out to be really traumatic because eight weeks from the date of leaving work he was in hospital having the toes on his left foot amputated.

This was to be the beginning of a long two years of operations culminating in the removal of both legs above the knees and a stroke which affected his eyesight. Now there had to be a total readjustment of our life.

Support from family and friends sustains you in your problems but I think there should be a period of rehabilitation for the disabled person. They are sent home to a caring family who naturally fuss and do everything for them. Then when the caring gets too much, as it usually does, or the carer gets ill, which happens, the disabled cannot manage because they have not had to cope alone. That is why I think a period of adjustment is very necessary for both the disabled and the carer. Most carers do not realise at the beginning that the disabled must find out what they are capable of doing.

I felt cheated and often very angry because information was always so difficult to obtain. There seemed to be a cloak of secrecy about what you should or should not have. E.g. leaflets are available for most things but so many leaflets! And when you think you have sorted out the ones which should apply to your case, you find they do not apply until a certain age, or within a certain income group.

Holidays present a big problem. You cannot just decide to take off into the blue. You have to find out if the wheelchair will go through the doors, will the bathroom and toilet have easy access? And will it be large enough? Are there stairs and if so how many? The list is endless, little things that present no problems to people in general. But to a carer with a wheelchair at times impossible.

Social life can be a problem. There are organisations to cope with the disabled and on their social occasions they are well catered for. They have carers in attendance and usually have a really good time. But visits to theatres or cinemas require the usual homework on access. It is understandable that all buildings cannot be built with wide doors and ramps, although new buildings have to conform with these regulations. We are finding every day more and more people in wheelchairs or other modes of transport wanting to participate in everyday life like the able.

Family opinions matter a great deal in caring for a disabled person. There can be quite a difference of opinion. Some might say 'He should do it himself' or it might be 'Do it for him, you know he cannot manage'. I think a happy medium has to be found. The ideal solution is one where the capabilities of the disabled must be assessed. They should not get the impression that everything is impossible. At least they should be allowed to try. In this way they will know their limitations and the carer will know how much is expected of them in terms of helping.

This idyllic situation is often a mere pipe dream of a carer. It has no real chance of succeeding because caring, really caring, cancels all thoughts of being hard and making them try.

Mr C. was trying very hard to keep his job. His wife had multiple sclerosis very badly and was unsafe to be left

alone at all. Community services were of little help – district nurse for half-an-hour each morning and a home help to prepare a midday meal. Eventually, he resigned from work. Within three months, his wife died. He now, at the age of forty-eight, feels that there is little chance of his ever being able to find another job.

PAT WATMAN

Pat and her husband live in the London Borough of Brent. Her mother, who is in her eighties, was cared for by her husband, until his death, and now lives with Pat. An aunt living nearby also requires a great deal of help now. Pat has appeared in a Channel 4 TV programme on the stresses of caring for an elderly mentally infirm relative.

A Carer's Eye View

The original carer in the family was my father, who started to look after my mother single-handed at home after she had a stroke in 1974. I would go along with my husband for about a day a week to help out and give Dad a break, but I couldn't do too much more at the time as my own health wasn't in the best shape. My father managed very well in fact but, after five solid years without a real break, his health began to suffer. In June 1979 I went over –with my long-suffering husband – to live at home and look after Mum, while Dad went into hospital for a relatively simple operation. We thought we would be there for a few weeks or even months, but less than a year later Dad died of cancer.

This was especially traumatic for me because I had in the

meantime become totally exhausted trying to look after Mum (a big enough job in itself), Dad when he was at home, a neglected house, a large garden, my husband and myself, our abandoned flat, and also give a lot of support to an elderly aunt – my mother's sister – who lives in a Home nearby. (Luckily I have no children!) When the crunch came and Dad, dying, desperately wanted to come home from hospital, I HAD to say no and I believe he died hating me for it, being unable – in his agony – to understand my predicament.

I couldn't even get to the hospital to be with him in his last hours because I couldn't find anyone (at very short notice) to look after Mum at the time. I didn't even have time to grieve properly. I just had to plough on as best I could, shocked and debilitated. Mum, too, was devastated as, not anticipating it myself, I hadn't been able to prepare her for his imminent death.

As the only child, I now had total responsibility for my mother and everything else. I felt at the time that I would probably go under within a few months, so exhausted had I become. Indeed I might have, had it not been for the support and help of my husband, despite his own demanding job, and an agency nurse who became a friend, grew to love my mother like her own, and shouldered the main burden with me at that time. (Fortunately we had that bit of extra money to be able to afford her!)

And so I became – unofficially – the carer. Luckily Mum was well enough, mentally and physically at that point, to walk a little by herself with the frame, and come downstairs with my help twice a day for meals and to watch TV. She could also get from her bedroom to the toilet by day and at night on to the commode by the bed under her own steam so that, although I dropped into bed sometimes so shattered that I couldn't even turn over to kiss my husband goodnight, I did at least get some sleep. (Also then I didn't have to lift her much and she was mostly continent.)

There were, however, innumerable problems – such as glaucoma, making her half blind, ill-fitting teeth and thus difficulty with eating, various aches and pains, a mouth infection – probably partly due to a night medicine. Having an inability to take pills myself I asked the doctor for a medicine, but couldn't find a suitable one. Then I got one which was easy to give and turned out to be a tranquilliser. Taking this over a few years led, I believe, to later problems of intense depression, but as I hadn't an easy alternative I kept her on them. The doctor, while willing, was, I think, not experienced enough to help me with these things. In the main I have found I have had to work things out for myself. Apart from this, Mum had been somewhat spoilt by Dad and wouldn't go to sleep until very late at night, keeping me up with her and persisting in all sorts of unnecessary habits which took a lot of time and energy to get her out of. I began a process of understanding what Dad had gone through.

In addition she was intensely nervous and when I left her on her own upstairs in the bedroom with a bell to call me for emergencies, she would ring it loudly time and time again for nothing – sometimes before I even got to the bottom of the stairs. The sound of that bell began to drive me and my husband mad.

At that time I was still trying to cope as well with big problems in the house (roof leaks, etc), my aunt, and all the rest. The only help I was getting then from the council was a district nurse to give Mum a weekly blanket bath and a home help, also once a week. We were still paying for the agency nurse and one or two other very helpful people and, as we needed lots of time off just to keep going, the bills were getting astronomical. If we hadn't had the money I would not have been able to carry on, but where then would Mum have gone? The social worker told us there was simply no place for Mum to go in our area. They had no facilities for someone who needed a little more care than they normally get in old people's homes (although she didn't really need *medical* care). They offered to take her into hospital to give me a break, but she didn't want to go.

However, I did put her in at one point. Looking back now

with more experience, it probably wasn't so bad, but when you look after a person at home both you and they come to expect too much. Also, as you want to visit, you take back washing (otherwise they tend to lose her clothes), it is not quite the rest it is supposed to be.

We also tried a couple of private homes, but they didn't work out very well. They also tend to be for the 'active elderly' and sometimes, with the best will in the world, they don't understand completely, and leave you with more problems than you put her in with. Mum hated them.

Time was passing. My health was deteriorating, our social life had come to a standstill, as I never had the energy to entertain, and my marriage was subjected to a lot of strain. I was beginning to get increasingly desperate. My home help was withdrawn (I never did find out why) and the nurse who helped me was going abroad for a while. I then tried advertising privately and got lots of replies. Here luck was with me and I found another wonderful lady who lifted the burden for a few hours a week and helped me personally a great deal – in practical ways, like doing my ironing, and emotionally by being a confidante and friend, while looking after Mum and my aunt when she came round with all her problems. Eventually I also got a 'Crossroads' lady from the social services to help out, although it was only four hours a fortnight, and much later on some help from the newly formed 'Triangle' organisation. I paid privately for a very nice home help.

But the strain was still enormous and Mum began to deteriorate slowly. Her mind began to go and she became more and more nervous (if that were possible) and less and less coherent. It became increasingly difficult to talk to her, so I just fed her and looked after her physical needs, but ignored her in other ways, particularly as I only had the energy to do the practical things and I couldn't answer her emotional needs as well.

At first I didn't understand her increasing dementia and thought she was just 'being difficult' – which made me angry.

Then again, the most soul-destroying aspect is the sheer inescapable *boredom* of it – not being able to communicate properly with her, or get her to do what you want logically. Few people can understand the sense of desperation, left alone for long periods with a confused elderly person, unless they have done it themselves. It makes you do and say cruel things even though you love the person. (I hadn't understood it myself when my own father did it.)

That's when it is dangerous. I loved her, but she unwittingly drove me to the brink – and over. Into violence.

At first it was just verbal, but then I started to hit her and pull her around and throw her on to the bed. My husband was upset and worried I might hurt her, of course – so was I. As he said, if I did do her harm I would never forgive myself. Though I couldn't stop it, I tried to control it insofar as I didn't hurt her badly but just tried to frighten her. It did that all right, but it didn't change anything and it couldn't have been doing me any good either.

Early in 1983 Mum contracted pneumonia and nearly died. But at 84 she's a tough little lady and she survived, though more impaired. She can no longer walk unaided, come downstairs or look after herself at night, and she's become increasingly incontinent and has problems with piles. However, the things that are really beginning to kill me now are the lifting (I haven't got the strength), being woken up at least two or three times every night – simply because 'There's no one there' or 'I thought it was time to get up' and the 'thumping'. I took away the bell, except at night, as she can't use it responsibly and I go to her frequently. But she doesn't understand and has developed a trick of banging on anything around to attract attention. It's her way of communicating. But night and day, I can't take it.

So now they've taken her into hospital again and finally, after I was getting into various states of exhaustion and beyond, they've agreed to take her in regularly on a month in, month out basis. Mum complained bitterly at having to go into hospital again, but I no longer felt as guilty as I would have done previously, since I know *I had no choice.* I try to explain that the choice is not between going into hospital or not going, but between going in permanently if I went under, or just temporarily so that I can still look after her some of the time at home.

The hard part is that when she's home the strain is physical, but when she's in hospital – where the care is basic because of overcrowding and staff shortages – the strain is emotional, but just as great. It makes me ill to see her there, try and cope with all the problems and hear her say 'Get me out of this madhouse' or 'You'll go home, I won't!'.

And so the story is not over yet. All I want now for myself is to get my health back and keep it – and that of my husband – in reasonable shape, so that 'one day when we're free' we will have an easier time and perhaps some strength left to live full lives again.

What I want for Mum is a relatively easy time of it for what there is left, because I can't bear to see her suffer, and before it gets too bad, an easy, merciful way out – peacefully at home, I hope, with me holding her hand.

I'm afraid, however, the reality on both those counts is likely to be very different. Now I know why Dad went under – and shall all my life believe that if he had had some real help and relief in his caring role, he would not have come to his end as soon as in the way that he did. I only hope the same doesn't happen to me – and all the countless other people like us, who take on what turns out to be an impossible task – FOR LOVE.

DAVID LEIGHTON

David L. is a professional man living in the North of England. He and his wife have two children and his wife has had two long periods of mental illness. At the time of

going to press she is very much improved. His experience is one of the things contributing to a great interest in healing.

Not long after my wife was first in hospital, when we had been married for about a year, I drove past a stretch of road where we had stopped together on our honeymoon. I got out of the car, walked up the embankment, and thought back to the year before. I was filled with a conviction that all was finished. It was over. There was no more hope. Yes, they assured me at the hospital, she would recover, and I believed them, but somewhere I knew that something had been irretrievably lost, some mutual trust between us, that sense of inner certainty we had had, that when we walked with each other we would relate in a sane and natural way, however tempestuous the exchange.

Many breakdowns since, I can now face that feeling and know that it is true some of the time, but that it is not true all of the time. We have learned ways together of living with the affliction, almost to be grateful for certain aspects of it, though never entertaining such stupid ideas like the one that mental illness is a more real form of living than any other. I can see the truth in that. People in all types of distress have said the same and I suppose any kind of survival takes you to the heart and essence of living. But that is very different from masochistically wanting it or supposing that the devastation which afflicts the family is desirable. It is not, and half the art of caring is ensuring that you and the family survive so that they are intact and the caring can continue.

How? A first way is to try and discover some meaning and purpose within it. One of the things which distresses my wife is that her illness might be ruining my life, and prospects, whatever they are. At times, when that devastating emotion self-pity takes hold, I sometimes feel the same, until I take it into my prayer. Prayer has been vital because it has forced me to face reality, to absorb the truths of all my wife says about me, especially the penetrating observations when she is held by the disease, to understand where all that is happening fits into the meaning and purpose of our lives. Life would become false if I were to suppose that the two of us could avoid or run away from this central fact of our lives. Somehow what happens is part of our overall being and purpose.

While on this spiritual side of the subject, a second essential is the requirement of permanent forgiveness. We do devastating things to each other in the stress and the strain, and we become so critical and angry in that peculiarly accurate probing way that couples who have grown to know and love each other are so painfully adept at. Mutual forgiveness is a continuing must; and understanding. I had in fact studied mental illness before my wife was first ill, so knew a little of what to expect, but if I had not, I would have devoured anything relevant there was. Everyone is casting around in the dark anyway, but it is a help to know this, to explore the various theories and above all to come to understand in some way what is happening to the person you love, how she ticks, how she is affected, and how you tick and are affected in response – and how you contribute by making it worse or – more happily – better.

Friends can be a wonderful help here. I have been peculiarly fortunate in having a number of friends or groups who have been prepared to hear me out and to bear with my one-sided account. There is no question that these are the people who are important, far more than the statutory services, much as you need them at different times. Friends may say the daftest things or offer the most ridiculous advice, yet you can hear the concern and are warmed by that. Nonetheless, good official helpers are an enormous help. Currently we are valuing the best experience we have ever had of a General Practitioner who is demonstrating real care. The security she gives us is a marvellous help. Such a contrast to those helpers who drag out information for their forms without looking at you, who trick you into giving some background information they want to support their latest theory or who cannot see that you too are distressed and that you may be tired and exhausted, yet seem to forget that you love your wife however angry you are and need a touch of empathy in the ghastly time.

When all is well – all is well. When things are going wrong the major pain is seeing it happen and having to adjust to a new relationship when the one person you want to share the sadness with is the person who is slipping away into another persona and cannot hear you. Yet, even in these terrible times we are together, and perhaps at the deepest levels – and at any level where the relationship can be maintained, in the physical bond of sexual intercourse, for example – the relationship grows and develops.

But sometimes it will be too much. Recently that was what was happening to me. Our efforts to maintain a normal life were failing, my temper was running out of control and I was becoming more and more exhausted and despairing. There is no room for heroes in caring and something had to be done. I struggled with the problems in silence, and in writing and in discussion with friends, and found there were two fairly simple practical steps I could take which might be helpful to both of us. For myself, I attended to my need for rest, arranged some outings to the theatre and settled down to think and pray my way through to some new boundaries, to draw up protective measures to help me withstand long aggressive verbal attacks, confused irrational discussions or plans which on first hearing sounded peculiarly threatening.

Supporting friends, ruthless realism and a struggle to understand, a reasonable degree of self-protection, and the caring moves from the stance of one caring for the other to a mutual sharing and journeying and an acceptance that though the manic-depression may always recur – holding on to the hope (not optimism) that it might not.

CAROL TURNER

Carol, another Essex contributor, has two disabled family members. Both her husband and her son have muscular dystrophy. Carol has been a carer for over thirty years.

What is it like to live with a disabled person? What a difficult question, it is so complex. My husband has muscular dystrophy, and in his case it has been a very slow process of deterioration. He also now has glaucoma, and has lost most of his sight, so his days are spent between bed and his wheelchair. He is a lovely man. We met and married when he was twenty-two and I was seventeen. His complaint had not yet been diagnosed, little was known about it then except that there is no helpful treatment.

People like me possibly know as much about it as anyone, as it is our experience that tells us it is hereditary and people probably live for a long time. We have four children and now four grandchildren. They are all married except my youngest and have moved to various parts of the country with their jobs, but we see them quite often and there is the telephone. My youngest son, now thirty, has known the affliction since he was ten. We had seen the signs a long time before then. The realisation was a very traumatic experience for us all, including our GP who had reassured me in my pregnancy that I had nothing to worry about. I am very grateful things are better now and no one need make our mistake. However, my son is absolutely marvellous – still able to walk – just about – and he will have a go at anything. So positive where my husband is completely negative. We all love music and my son is exceptionally talented. Through this he has made a life for himself with lots of good friends. I get a lot of fun from being a part of the local operatic society.

How much I have contributed to my husband's long life I

do not know, but I do not think I have done anyone any favours.

My little granddaughter said to me the other day, 'My friend Katie's Grandad died and her Granny got a new one – couldn't you do that, Granny?' 'What a good idea', we all cried, 'but I don't think Grandad would like it somehow do you?' The ultimate throw-away society. Sick humour? Well this is how we are, I am afraid. It enables us to express the perfectly natural, but perhaps socially unacceptable, thoughts we have. I find writing down them and later tearing them up helps too. I am appalled at the waste everywhere. It's a vicious circle in a way. We get better but by no means adequate payments which involve us to care for people at home. They are better cared for at home (cheaper, but at what cost to the carer?), for you have to be really strong to be in hospital any time. What with the food and the infections, not to mention the odd experimental operations – a person may die! But at home – well! There is twenty-four-hour personal service, TV, visitors all hours, fancy food. No messing about with people changing shifts or going on holiday. No doctor or anyone comes to bother you – why, you can even – quite legitimately – get fresh with the nurse as she hangs about, whether she likes it or not! Certainly you can stop her having any fun and games by just, simply always being there. Great! A person could live forever. It's been almost forty years and it's not going to get any better, I'm afraid, not for me anyway. There seems no way I can recharge my batteries. I would like to see centres set up where long-term home patients would have to go every so often for a complete medical check up. Their financial situation gone through to see if they are getting everything they should. As many as possible of the aids available for them to try and order there and then. This would give the carer a break without her or him having to 'push' it. There are so many aids which can only be got through a social worker or someone and, with the best of intentions, it is often pretty hit and miss. When my husband could still walk a little, he used to use my garden hoe as a 'staff'. It was light and you could use it from any hand position. Great!

Someone from social services thought a wheeled frame would be better, despite our denials. It had to be ordered especially from Dublin and when it arrived six weeks later it would not go through the door. It was enormous! I thought of using it as a frame for my beans and tomatoes. We telephoned 'Please come and take it away' – social services were most upset. Someone came and jubilantly exclaimed 'It's not the frame that's too big. The house is too small and unsuitable!' (Never mind I couldn't move it, let alone an invalid. Plus we had just moved into this house!) We had spent all our married lives in 'temporary dwellings'. These are places bought by the council to demolish to make way for new estates or roads, whatever, so we never knew how long we would be able to live there or where we would be allocated – for thirty years!!

Time again we would see younger couples with fewer children, able-bodied people who could live anywhere they chose, move into the new properties but somehow we never qualified, until the new high-rise estates came in, with a section of especially built flats for disabled people. When I made a fuss, we were offered one, which I refused as I maintained we were an ordinary family who happen to have a disabled person to cater for. 'Thank you, but I believe we have as much right to choose as the next and I would like a house.' I have come to the conclusion the authority solves the problems of adapting a house to suit an invalid by simply never allowing the invalid to be allocated a house in the first place. I appealed to our MP and everyone I could think of. We were advised to try and exchange but since we were not in 'permanent accommodation' this was difficult. However, we set up three separate exchanges, including one to be nearer my mother. All were turned down. There was no obligation to give a reason why.

We had solved the financial problem, when my husband could no longer go to work, by swapping jobs. He was to stay home and do what he could and just be there when the children came home. I became a 'clippie'. This gave us a 'man's wage' for the odd hours of work, which sometimes saw me home finished (in all senses) before the family were up. I got clothes and all sorts of marvellous people to work with. Thus our children were able to stay on for higher education.

When they left school (some to be married and away), I left the job and eventually became a home help. A mistake. I should have taken sick leave; I was extremely tired and menopausal. Alas, the job no longer exists, neither do my dear friends. I realise now, too late, that I should have notified the council of our changed circumstances, asked to have the tenancy put in my name, as breadwinner. The tenant was a disabled unemployed man with four children, on paper, no wonder we got substandard places – I leave you to work out the ethics of that. I saw these houses one day on our way to the Shaftesbury Society Mission here. Nice quiet street near the park, two bedrooms up, two rooms down (one could be used as a bedroom), bathroom, toilet and kitchen downstairs. Big garden (grow our own vegetables, somewhere private to sit out), lovely neighbours. Great!

Suddenly we were offered one. We had to be in in one week, we were told, and this is where our Social Services friend came in.

We would have to move soon as the houses were to be modernised, completely overhauled and given a bathroom upstairs. We would be given special consideration and all we had to do was to be moved out to somewhere suitable temporarily. It was to be a specially adapted house for a person of limited mobility with an open-plan downstairs and a wheel-in shower. Where would he sleep – in the bath!!! My husband's request to go into care while the work was done was met with incredulous silence and then agreement, but we would be found somewhere suitable so do not worry! The difficulty of moving twice with someone in our condition brought little sympathy – plans are plans. My request to be helped to move near to one of my children was declared impossible. After waiting some weeks to be offered something I still refused to consider a flat.

I became extremely depressed. My son suggested we asked how much it would cost under the 'right to buy' scheme and this we have done. We hope for completion soon. So here we are again amidst the ruins of the other houses and gardens – but we shall not be moved! Please God! My friends and neighbours come each day like 'homing pigeons' to clean and inspect the re-building.

When fifteen-year-old John's mother became ill with cancer, he undertook most of her nursing care. She died within a matter of weeks, leaving him to look after his father. Mr D. is in his seventies, blind, deaf and totally dependent. The only contact John has had with a potential source of help was shortly after his mother's death, when a social worker called to see how he was coping. He has seen no one since.

MARIE FREEMAN

Marie, in her late forties lives in the Home Counties, and cares for John, one of her six children, who was badly injured in a motor bike accident four and a half years ago. In a court case relating to the accident, the Judge commended Marie's devoted and outstanding care for her son, which had returned him to a degree of normality which would never have been predicted.

No one is indispensable, yet for a brain-damaged, handicapped person, certain members of the family are indispensable, simply because it is from them that they learn to rebuild their lives again, like a child placing all its trust on the mother, so this is what John has done to me, and the rewards have been great.

John, at the age of 18 years old, was pillion riding on a friend's motor bike when he was in collision with a car one Sunday night. John and Ian, his friend, were both seriously injured. In John's case amongst other damages was brain damage, which was operated on twice, first twelve hours after the accident, then approximately four months later. He was in a coma for eleven months; then, after fifteen months, I was asked if I'd have him home. There was never any doubt in my mind, but I did wonder if I would be capable of looking after him. I realised that if I did have him home it would be a twenty-four-hour job. There would be no social life, no freedom to come and go as I pleased.

The early days of John coming home seem nowadays to be one span of six months, where the first three months I slept on the settee alongside his bed until I knew his sleeping habits, and was able to go upstairs to bed, and I had taught him how to ring a bell. I also taught him to eat properly with a fork and spoon. It seemed that no sooner he'd have finished eating one meal, than I had to turn round and get another meal ready. Also during that first six months my other sons and daughters were always available to care for him if I needed their help.

Paul, the youngest, used to come home at lunch time and help me lift him into a low reclining armchair at 1 o'clock, and the physio and I used to put him on the floor about 3 p.m. and she'd work on his hands, legs and arms for an hour each day and every day of the week, till we got his legs flexible and his arms and back stronger. Today he can pull himself up with his arms around any member of the family and stand for a minute or two. I learned how to bath him myself, and as John gained knowhow and strength into his legs so I found ways of lifting him myself and within a year, John and I were independent of others, yet others were there to help if need be.

By the end of the first year, John could wash his face and hands and clean his teeth in about three quarters of an hour.

Today it takes him ten minutes. Also there was the blending of his food, particularly meat; this Christmas he complained that the slices of meat were not big enough! He butters his own bread, and the paralysed hand he is now using more and more. I took John to a handicapped class for typing, and in two years he learned all the skills of a typist except the speed. He now has an English tutor who comes one evening a week, and is using the typewriter for his lessons.

I intend now to find a voice tutor to help with speech, as a speech therapist does not seem to meet his need. Words are there and John is quite able to talk. What he needs is a voice therapist to help him learn to project his voice, and there is a possibility that we'll also engage a tutor to give him a refresher course on the guitar.

For the past year and a half I have been taking John to hydrotherapy on Thursday morning and to a private swimming bath on Monday afternoons. When we started it took three of us to walk John across the pool; twelve months later John can walk across the pool with my help only. All this has taken long, patient effort and will power on John's and my part. John has the determined will to do these things, and I have somehow gained the patience to help him.

Looking after someone with a head injury is different from looking after a child, an elderly relative or even a handicapped person who was born that way. Usually a head injury who succeeds enough to go home, goes home because there is no more the hospital can do to help, and in all cases the head injury improves because they are in the environment of their own family, and like most people, feel secure. But so far to date there is a lot to be done and a lot to be learned about head injuries by most hospitals. Even today doctors cannot tell me about John, as to whether he'll improve more or not. Fundamentally his injuries are the same, a part of the damaged brain was removed and therefore can never be replaced, only other cells can be made to work, and that will depend on how much determination John has left. According to medical science, the brain continues to develop until a person is twenty-five years old and if that is so, then John has at least two and a half years to go.

Help from Social Services, etc. is poor, simply because John is the reverse of what is generally needed. Cheshire Homes are about the only group homes available to the likes of people like John. In our case it is a task of re-education. There is nothing in our locality, but if one is prepared to look and engage private help it is there. It was daily private physiotherapy that got John started and as he is today. I have the help of the local hospital physio and hydro now that John is allowed to go swimming, but it took over a year to get the doctor to give permission for John to go into the water.

It was me who found out whether John could cope with the water. I took him into a pool on a holiday for disabled people in Jersey, then came back here in 1982 and insisted that John would benefit from hydrotherapy.

The caring of a head injury at home put a tremendous strain on the family. In our case we had to give up a sitting room to become John's bedroom and dayroom. There is a very strong bond between myself and all the children (there are five others). John's accident and homecoming, and his recovery, have brought much strain to all members, and from the beginning it affected them all. Jeremy, the eldest, now twenty-seven and schizophrenic long before the accident, experienced great jealousy, and took an overdose. He was lucky, and is well and happy today, and getting married later in the year. Anne, now twenty-six years old, was married and got divorced, and I couldn't give her the comfort she needed, but during the early years and the eleven months of John's coma, she shared the long hours of looking after John, talking to him, reading, taking him out, releasing me for a break each day, during the eight hours I spent daily at John's bedside. Michael is now aged twenty-four years. As much as John was his favourite brother, it 'broke his heart', and he could not stand to see John in the coma, so went to live in Jersey with my brother. But he had the joy of asking John to be his best man at his wedding last August. John turned it down, understandably, but if he were asked today, he'd say yes, I'm sure of it. Helen, aged twenty-one years now, like Anne, was a tower of strength, went out and learned to drive as soon as she was eligible, passed her test, then took me everywhere, and was responsible for bringing John home each weekend, then when John was home, and I could not leave him to go shopping. Helen did all the family shopping until recently, and took time off work to drive John and myself to the regular visits to the hospital. Helen was also responsible for getting the dinner five nights a week while I was at the hospital during those early months. Paul, now nineteen, is still at home and still helps out with various duties as and when they occur.

There was lots of mistrust from John and there still is a little, and there was a lot of resentment from the children, as a whole, over silly little things that were nevertheless important at the time, because they felt I devoted so much time to John. Yet they understood, and were so forgiving in their understanding.

John, on the other hand, went through terrible fits of frustration. The inability to express himself gave way to temper, clawing, biting, pinching, whoever was near enough to be the victim! This suddenly started up in the second year of being home. It was difficult to understand him, he'd throw whatever was near, dinner, plates, cutlery, anything, then eventually I started to react back to him at one stage. My arms were a mass of cuts, bruises, pinches and so on. But we won the day and it paid off, John learned the vital lesson of behaviour, just like a small child who goes off in a tantrum because it cannot have its own way.

We have just had a marvellous Christmas where John wholeheartedly took part in everything, whereas in other years since the accident John hated even a Christmas card, and would not share me with the others. He bought beautiful presents. I spent two whole days taking John round the shops Christmas shopping, and though he almost walked the feet off me, I would not have missed it for the world, seeing him taking his own money out of his wallet and paying for his purchases. That was just one of the many many rewards in this 'long game' of recovery.

I would never want to go through this again, but the experience I have had, the joy of seeing life rekindled again from the first time the eyes opened, and I told the nurse, she replied 'you imagined it' but apologised three days later, as she'd seen it herself, to tonight when John pulled himself up on a chair, the laughter that followed because he'd done it four and a half years later, is an unspeakable experience. To strive for the impossible, to have faith and trust to live for today, let tomorrow take care of itself.

The adventures, the first plane flight, the holidays – there is so much. Life, like the plant that almost dies, if you take the little bit that's left and nurture it with love and care, who knows what you may be rewarded with. Perhaps, like me, you'll find the greatest gift this earth can give, a full life again.

Today I drive – I take John everywhere, it took five tests before I passed my test. We go shopping, visiting, and attend various functions, meet people, and have people home here. John is taking Third Year, approximately, English with his tutor, he enjoys it, does 'homework'. Who knows – he may in five years or so re-take English 'O'-level. His intelligence is high, he enjoys conversation, speaks his mind, has a good musical ear, is not content to be idle, has discovered an art called liquid embroidery, and is busy painting cheeky pictures on his new t-shirts this week.

This is the boy who at eighteen years old and after an accident was given a life of a possible 98 per cent cabbage if he came out of the coma.

DOREEN HORE

Doreen is a professional woman, now in her late fifties, who brought up three children as well as looking after her parents, during which time her marriage broke up.

Her parents have both died since she wrote this piece and she is trying to resume active life in the North-East of England. Her favourite occupation at the moment is belonging to a number of choirs.

We are all beset by fears and anxieties about elderly relatives. Will it get much worse? Will I be able to cope? How long will it last? What happens afterwards?

Birth is a natural process. It can be planned and there is a time limit: not so with death. It may be taboo to discuss it, but the only ultimate release for the carer is the death of the patient.

Chance has spared me nursing Mother to her death at eighty-four. Last week I took her to a local authority home for a fortnight's holiday relief – the first available since nursing Father five months ago, when he came out of holiday care to die. The next day she suffered a massive stroke, total brain damage and has remained unconscious. Her kidneys and heart, weak at forty, still haven't given out. Physically she has been well-cared for and could have lasted indefinitely, devoid of quality of life. Thankfully, she is being allowed to die. Our caring society puts down its pets, whilst preserving people and glibly asserts that we don't die 'before our time has come'.

Surgeons re-plumbed Father, for another forty-two years of man-given life, in a drastic experimental sub-total gastrectomy and duodectomy, without even preliminary X-ray. Eventually it resulted in unrecognised vitamin B12 deficiency, only treated latterly after collapse into intensive care. Every survival day was spent in apprehension, agony or pure bile sickness or even a semi-coma with a 'seized' digestion, relieved only by drops of whisky, hot drinks and hot water bottles. Feeding him was a perpetual anxiety and he dare not eat out. He also suffered an orchidectomy, through related poisoning, it was said. Also an 'urgent' waterworks job was accomplished after three years of clerical blundering. In addition he had arteriosclerosis, Reynaud's disease, emphysema, deafness since a First War gun explosion, double cataracts and had broken his neck, pelvis and toes. But he could use toilet paper, so was refused even a day care allowance from the health gnomes of Blackpool, twice, despite medical recommendation for 'post-operative syndrome'. Thus I looked after two for the price of one. Now the pioneer Newcastle Council for the Disabled exists to fight appeals. As Mother's condition became more demanding, he became more frail and sick yet received less attention.

Thirty years ago I carried parents' meals-on-wheels in my infant's pram as I came to do their heavy gardening, cleaning and decorating. Then followed a decade of psychiatric nursing. A prematurely-senile cousin lived with me at one stage. When she had to move out I was then running three households and seven persons. I lost my sons to boarding-school, then my home when my marriage came to a violent and abrupt end. My parents took me in. Since they were already disabled – mother severely arthritic then – I didn't have much option. Not being gainfully employed, I have always been available for exploitations – for that is what care in the community means – the willing horse does the work. Eventually one becomes embittered when one's own health suffers and there is no escape from the duty one did out of love.

Indeed, it is circumstances, not vocation, that condemns us to bottom-washing. Personally I rejected nursing as a career, which is a pity, for I have spent my life doing it. Yet, had I trained I could have achieved the status that absolved me from menial tasks in maturity, too professionally committed to nurse my own; and yet, as a salary-earner, I would have been able to enjoy the privilege of falling sick, having a private life, whole weekends off, statutory holidays and an index-linked pension in two years' time.

My cousin had Huntington's chorea. She had been a teacher, social worker and publisher. Realising residential resources were so inadequate as to be available only on a rota basis and the 'community' had failed totally to support her outside, she committed suicide in a spirit of self-euthanasia. She was right, of course. I found her dead. A homeless schizophrenic patient had been discharged to her home as resident domestic. She lay in bed in a perpetual menopausal mess until evening without even boiling an egg, until my cousin felt like murdering her and appealed to me to remove her. The authorities had solved their over-crowding problem by increasing her anxiety and doubling my workload. Only at the post-mortem did I discover community nurses existed.

Lack of liaison is tragic as well as deplorable. Staff should not assume senile patients can relay messages to relatives, whatever their IQ, for their minds are like jigsaws with the pieces falling apart, and short-term memory fallible.

Once my cousin arrived unheralded, on my doorstep, for the weekend. The psychiatric unit had consulted *her* if it was convenient. She had no food or aired bed in her own flat and only 50p in her possession.

However, now Newcastle Social Services deserves commendation for pioneering carers' support groups where one gets to know the relatives' social worker as a lifeline to whom one can address personal appeal in faceless bureaucracy. By exchanging experiences and ideas a guide to facilities has been published, for carers exist in isolation, with little opportunity to run round finding out. All the patients were referred from the department of geriatric medicine clinics, so various specialist speakers on incontinence, senility, Alzheimer's disease, etc. have been illuminating. Ideally, of course, carers should be caught before this stage, when they struggle alone. A video home nursing course to attend would be a great boon. Professionals do not realise we are essentially amateurs.

It is not easy to be on duty twenty-four hours a day caring for two patients with opposite requirements and totally unsynchronised routines. Father rested in bed after breakfast every day and if well enough was fed frequently; otherwise he lay for hours until the pain passed and often was alert at night. He was bedfast before injections with fatigue and afterwards with reaction, thus losing one week in every three. Mother ate like a horse, kept infant routine, rose early, fell asleep in the chair and retired to bed early, demanding Father did likewise and denied him television and me, music.

Worry induced her hypertension, frequent blackouts and nose bleeding. Excellent digestion and inactivity created obesity until I could not encompass her waist with both arms. Fear of doctor's wrath at not dieting kept her away from the surgery until pain of the osteo-arthritic knees drove her there. Esbatol prolonged her life beyond the family stroke/heart/dropsy mid-sixty death age until, with navy-blue extremities, she took her previous stroke around eighty and I was left nursing her single-handed for three months, granted a full-time attendance allowance and a weekly bath attendant.

Mother was left with asphasia, realisation that her last enjoyment, playing the piano, had vanished, total lack of motivation apart from obsessive toilet trips when frequently she couldn't find her way nor remember how to negotiate sitting on it, nor even how to sit in a chair. She had complete inability to dress and care for herself, loss of sense of time and mostly was unable to obey instructions to motivate her limbs, hampered anyway by arthritis. I did manage to retrain her to know her name, speak and eat with minimal assistance. She often thought I was her sister. She would abandon her zimmer and cling to the wallpaper pattern for support, or step off the wheelchair foot-rests if not strapped in or the foot-rests swung round. Aware she could not see, she couldn't connect it with spectacles nor put them on. Her sole remembered skill was buttoning and tying bows so she tried to tie shoes occasionally putting two on one foot. Latterly, when tired, she retained liquids in her mouth until she choked and only responded to persistent repetition of 'Now swallow!' to drink at all, until I felt like screaming. Her hearing remained acute and her former memory excellent. Geriatrics are demanding to live with, like perpetual toddlers with progressive regression, not improvement, who in panic, follow one everywhere, even to the toilet. One ceases to communicate since comprehension is negligible and dreads even mentioning going out lest they are down the steps, unattended, before we are ready. Exhausted relatives cannot stimulate the housebound. It is a situation without hope. Only social workers have it and one learns to appreciate their youthful exuberance as a contribution.

Daily attendance at the geriatric clinic followed the stroke and a three-week german measle type rash (drug withdrawal, presumably). Abrupt discharge ensued and diuretics have deflated her now to seven and a half stone from nearly fourteen.

Pushing and manoeuvring Mother damaged my five-foot-two skeleton so I now have an arthritic hip and permanent sciatica. Craving relief and supported by her general practitioner and mine, I asked for her to go into care; but patient's rights are paramount. A geriatric team doctor asked my semi-senile mother if she wanted to remain in her own home. Naturally she said 'yes', so couldn't be put on the waiting list – problem solved – one more permanent candidate for community care. Instead, she was offered day hospital twice weekly, effectively from 10 a.m.-3 p.m. depending on the ambulance route: not that I was free, with Father still to nurse.

I was refused home help because I was the resident daughter and the furniture was 'too big and heavy'. When my parents were my age it took three of us to maintain this modest bungalow and quarter-acre garden, yet I have had to do it alone whilst nursing two registered disabled geriatrics. Moreover, we lived at great inconvenience for months as it was being modernised, without grants, for their safety and comfort at my expense. With reluctance to assist owner-occupied dwellings, the council eventually installed a hand rail to three outside steps when private contractors failed to turn up for me.

I knew I was trapped. Thereafter I became resentful of the system and eventually of parents' lifelong expectations of me as an only child, not to mention their complacency, since their marriage and life-style was being perpetuated at my expense.

Had I remained in my own home there would have been no

problem. Their house would have been sold to keep them in care until such time as funds were exhausted, then care would have been free and my health wouldn't have suffered. Had they lived in a council house it wouldn't have been my concern either, for I would have walked out, leaving them to be transferred automatically. But owner-occupiers are different, as council purchasers would do well to consider. Having made my home in THEIR home I had no rights of tenure other than remain accident free to nurse them until I dropped or pay for their nursing care. Even transferring ownership could be construed as fraud unless accomplished within a given time limit (variable according to interpretation) of needing care. Of course the owner must be compos mentis. Any social security would cease until reinstated, if at all. For eight years the financial anxiety of losing my home if I couldn't escape, or having to re-mortgage my birthright on their deaths to retain it if I failed to pay for years of care for both of them has been hanging over my head and worrying Father who couldn't opt to relieve me. Nor would the local authority have taken into consideration the capital I invested in modernising a home in their name. The current rate for weekly care was £102 per person – £204 for two! So Father's death in a way lifted half my apprehension and Mother's death will bring security.

It is pertinent to point out that in the bad old days when grandmother was hospitalised for twelve years with Huntington's chorea she was no more confused than mother after a stroke – but not crippled and twelve years younger when she died – yet my mother dutifully visited her weekly with Thermos tea, never had to scrape her faeces from the carpet with a palette knife before breakfast and inherited this establishment from her father without hindrance – free at twenty-nine!

My parents' different assessments necessitated different care establishments, one with a weekend intake and the other mid-week reception, thus reducing my fortnight's break effectively to a week. There was no one else to visit them.

Carers cannot really make plans. I gave four months' notice

to get both my parents away so I could attend a 21st. I returned to visit and had to repeat the 200-mile journey for a wedding the following weekend, returning to bring Father home to die, still on my holiday. Mother's day hospital, meanwhile, has had a whole week off at Easter, another at Whitsun (and is due a fortnight in school holidays). Given funds, they would willingly take another forty patients and stagger hours to include evenings and weekends. Ambulance attendants have been short staffed and scrambling to get in annual leave before Easter. Yet, on my first Sunday off in five months, Mother started to die.

There is something wrong with a system that forces carers to their limits – for I am under no illusion, had she not actually been in authority care, a bed would not have been forthcoming since she was expected to be hospitalised last time.

My parents had no conception that divorce was bereavement and I was unable to remake my life in any respect. My sons had grown up, taking exams elsewhere where they could concentrate, graduated and moved away, regarding me also as a species of geriatric through living in permanent airless confinement with depressing bowel-orientated invalids, starved of exercise and mental stimulation.

In my late fifties, on the death of two contemporary friends, I decided parents' needs must be kept in perspective with mine for survival and the necessity to lay foundations for future aloneness (that they had never experienced). I resolved to treat caring as a job, like professionals do. Already in one choir, I accepted invitations to join another two, leaving Mother and Father at home together, for although frail, Father could summon help. So, on his death, I had a circle of friends who could sit for the other choir, so to speak, and I had somewhere to go and be welcomed. With them I started to learn to swim on day centre days of new freedom. At least I have support in my further changed existence, although I have no direction to pursue.

All my apprehension is engulfed by relief. Organising

another funeral is an incidental. The joy of having only myself to feed and consider will take some adjustment after all these years.

Certainly there is no daughter to sacrifice and tend to me, nor a place in an institution unless it is planned now. As for the future, I am resigned to remaining alone. Marriage prospects are limited to old gentlemen for whom I would, once more, become a carer.

ANNA BRIGGS

Anna comes from the north east and lives now on the Isle of Iona, as part of the community there. She and Brian have five children. Since writing this Brian has died, cared for at home by Anna.

The first operation was the day the Falklands were invaded. After nearly three months of going to the GP with severe arm pain and being given pain killers, my husband went to casualty. There they X-rayed and found, not a broken arm, but an extremely degenerated humerus. They must have had a fit when they saw the X-ray. The registrar, whom the probably panicking casualty doctor sent for, instituted some 'tests' straight away. For three days I could not imagine what *for*, because B. gave no hint of the questions he had been asked. He had answered 'no', truthfully, to all their cancer-symptom questions, so did not think he should mention them. After the tests, which made him depressed and as institutionalised as if he had *been* in hospital, I urged him strongly to go away to our favourite place in Scotland. The registrar, a Hindu, 'let' him go. (Later he said that he had B. down for immediate admission but understood that five days in this place would more than offset five days' delay in treatment.) Alarm bells began to ring for me when the ward sister phoned the day before he was due back, to ask why he had not admitted himself. I said it was the first I knew about admission. She realised she had gaffed and tried to cover her tracks.

When B. came back we had a lovely night together – it reminded me of the night our daughter was born and we brought her straight out of hospital after two hours. It was like a cocoon. But I remember thinking – the rest of our lives will never be the same.

One surgeon put a 'pin' (in reality a very large nail) through the humerus on 2nd April, and then (at a psychologically bad moment for both of us) called me into Sister's office for the 'serious talk with his wife'. He told me what he had already told B. This included the memorable phrase 'We may be facing the possibility of a short life' and the 65-year-old consultant was visibly shaken when I replied that we were all doing that. I was struck by the difference between his attitude and that of the Hindu registrar. He claimed to be a 'religious man' and obviously saw religion as a prop for bad times. The Hindu understood what I, a Christian, understand, that faith informs your whole existence.

Four days after the arm operation B. had recovered well enough, to everyone's amazement, to be taken back into theatre and have the primary removed – the right kidney. This had showed no symptoms, so came as a great surprise – but at least it was out. The kidney surgeon's houseman said the operation had been completely successful. I still feel strange about the fact that the man who cut up my lover's body never saw fit to even introduce himself to me – the person who had to nurse that body back to humanity.

Though we don't watch telly at home, the hospital thought that the least someone in B.'s condition needed was a portable TV by the bed. So all through our personal crisis a Ruritanian melodrama was being played out – 'The task force is still steaming to the South Atlantic'. It was only when B. came out of hospital and started to recover from the operation and the heavy radiotherapy on his arm that the war started for real. I certainly found out who my friends were when B. was in hospital – and I learned I had to avoid some people as well. Four people from a group I'm in put themselves (as well as their cars) at my disposal (we are car-less by choice). They would come in at the end of visiting, drive me home, ply me with wine and let me talk for hours. Another friend from the same group, who worked in the hospital B. was in, insisted on driving me 200 miles to a conference I had been going to go to. We drove back in the evening, called in to say goodnight to B. and she took me home. Fantastic! You sometimes need someone to take you over, to steer you in a crisis. My sons were very good – though they didn't say much; the eldest in particular took over the care of his younger sister and brother. One of my sisters sat with me while B. was in theatre – very valuable. But my other sisters and many close adults seemed unable to cope at all and I got waves of distress from them. Some of B.'s male contemporaries emerged from the woodwork to look at him and then went back again. I suppose they had to check it out – it could happen to them. I spent hours on the phone and began to feel like a recorded message – I joked about making one, or taking a page on Ceefax – and I spent as much time calming other people down as being calmed by them. I learned that someone else's crisis is worse than your own, partly because when you are in it, you go on to automatic pilot. Only later do you realise what was happening. Some important things kept me 'earthed' – the friends, the wine, having a very cuddly two-year-old still breast feeding, to comfort me at night. I don't know what comforted B. alone in his stiff hospital bed.

The day we came home was amazing – he filled such a big gap in the house (he's 6 feet 4 inches tall) and I began to feel everything would be all right again. Looking back on that, I feel incensed about the lack of useful information from the hospital. Though they were all (except the Hindu) into making big prognostications of one sort or another, they neglected day-to-day things. They gave us *no* notice of B.'s discharge – they told us nothing about likely recovery time from the kidney operation, from the radiotherapy – nothing about when to seek pain control, nothing about what treatment would affect B.'s fertility or libido. I realised that the first consultant, in orthopaedics, knew little about cancer, and that the prediction of the second, the 'kidney' man, that B. would be completely better and back to work in twelve weeks, was going to prove wildly wrong. The radiotherapist, when we eventually got to him, was dismissive of B.'s need to know about fertility.

The healing came from elsewhere. From our two stays in our favourite place later that year – from the support of fellow members of a community which believes in wholeness as the aim of healing rather than 'magic cures', from the opportunity – completely unexpected – to re-assess what we were doing with our lives together.

In what sense am I a carer? To some people I look freer – and in some ways I am – now we're together at home, rather than rushing off in different directions all day. There are some things we always both did – painting walls/changing light-bulbs/gardening, etc. – but it does make a difference to me, knowing that B. can't do anything involving lifting his right arm, and it is difficult to plan. From day to day because he can crash into pain and depression making it difficult for him to do anything and then on a longer scale – because two small bone secondaries appeared earlier in the year, giving the lie to the kidney team's predictions that there would be no more now the primary was gone. With both, B. had to refer himself, and this year, two consultants have said to him, 'We're going to keep a close eye on you from now on' and proceeded not to send him an appointment for months. There are some ways in which I'm like all carers – the 'if' of everyday living, only being able to do other things if B.'s not feeling bad about going out, even if he will be perfectly all right, partly because he's lost his status and role (his job), whereas I still have mine through my numerous unpaid activities, partly because I fear coming home and finding him slumped in a chair in pain and depression. There's the anger, which is good but difficult to express, about the way 'the condition' sometimes seems to be taking over everything else in the household. There's the feeling that my own aches and pains aren't important. This is partly I think why I got this latest bout of flu so badly – because B. *was* well enough to take care of me while I lay in bed. I think he did too. Part of what they call the 'scenario' is that I will outlive B. which is statistically likely but not guaranteed. A major part of keeping our relationship alive as a marriage, not as a carer-dependant situation, is to keep fighting these tendencies when they occur. Through some awful rows about them we have managed to stay in touch, indeed are more in touch than we ever were before. It is wonderful for me to see how his authority has blossomed when talking to other people about healing. Layers of pain, peeled off, have revealed a powerful and deeply thinking and feeling person.

We have had to come to terms with the fact that doctors are not going to save his life – only he can save himself, with the support he needs from others. In fact, he is at his worst around the time of a hospital appointment. He becomes, for a time, a sick patient again, re-enlivening for a short time by now dead fantasy that the hospital was only lending him back to me. There is no way of knowing whether the attitude he picks up from doctors is because they think he'll get better anyway, they couldn't care less, they are snowed under with work/the cuts. Though their acute treatment last year was technically excellent, you begin to see the shabby fabric of the health service in a deprived region. They have a whole body scanner, donated after an emotional public fundraising effort – and not enough people to staff it.

The worst day ever was when we saw two consultants, one before lunch, one after. They had obviously argued about the course of treatment in the lunch-hour, and we got the backwash from the second. He was brusque, if not rude. We had wanted to go and see the film *Gandhi* that afternoon, but had been persuaded to see the second consultant instead. We should have gone to see *Gandhi*.

So B. is looking to the alternatives. Special diets are socially difficult – imagine eating raw carrot when your family are tucking into a steaming plate of curry or chili con (soya) carne! The thing that will get him there will be the healing network we are in, and we have discovered the sacramental healing of sexuality – from early after the operations I have wanted him to know his body is just as beloved (more so, if anything) and not, to me, scarred and disfigured. When a man has been ill that can lead to problems – you take the risk of reinforcing feelings of impotence. Like everything else, sex is a sensitive plant that needs careful tending. There are some things I dread. When the pain gets worse in one of the tumour sites – that's awful, because as a headachy person myself, I know a bit what it's like to be in constant pain and I dread meeting people whose first question is 'how's B.?' I've checked myself out – I think when I meet people in different circumstances I try not to ask THE question about the circs or to wait till it leads itself out – as it surely does. If the sufferer, or the carer, does not want to talk about it, that's their privilege. Last week I went to a conference where the first three people that spoke to me asked THAT question. The third was amazed when I bit her head off. I feel as if I'm being cast as the Brave Cancer Patient's Wife. In here, it doesn't feel like that most of the time. It's a bit like visualisation techniques – you have to see your strong body conquering a tiny tumour. We have to see our strong lives and loves, conquering (whatever the outcome) a specific condition. B. says some people make him feel as if he was dying. The people in our community don't do that to him. He is involved in the rough and tumble – and therefore feels totally normal.

I made a promise to myself early on. Whatever happens, he won't end up in hospital – whatever the cost. Life is a process, and you only have one chance to do things right. Dying is as important a part of that process as living. I have a few teachers about doing it right, especially two women who have lost children into death or permanent handicap. I told some medical students at a meeting this year that how you experience a crisis is just as important as whether you survive it. They were shocked – but I still meant what I said. Doctors have to take their cues from us, about the meaning of what we are experiencing – and not vice versa. We have to live – and die – our own lives.

I fantasise more than I used to. Sometimes I wake up and I've dreamed B.'s funeral – even the hymns. Another time (as today, after a bad bout of flu and fever) I woke up thinking I'd dreamed it all, that he was really OK. Of course the reality lies in the middle, as usual. I've learned a lot about our screwed-up society and its screwed-up priorities. I've thought about the mothers and wives of the 'disappeared' in Latin America. Where am I on their scale of suffering? For our own experience, the poem by Tessa Ransford best sums it up:

HOSPITALISATION*

Illness tossed you over the rails
of our world –
The huge hospital swallowed you
then swam away
to go through its routines with you
deep and distant.

I could no more than paddle in
that element –
but came often to watch from the shore
and scan the surface.

After a secret number of days
and hidden nights,
after fathomless hours enclosed
in the whale's belly
floating on tides of attention
and murmurs of movement,
the hospital will spit you out again
at my feet.

*'Hospitalisation' is reprinted by permission of Tessa Ransford and The Ramsay Head Press, 36 North Castle Street, Edinburgh EH2 3BN from her book of poems entitled *Light of the Mind*.

The sand is suddenly swept with
scuttling pebbles
sprays of scum and shells
as you come up on it.
I begin to lead you home, only
to discover
we are on a foreign shore.

This has been all about learning to live on that shore.

Mrs B. was abandoned by her husband in 1982, and left to cope with her severe disability alone. Her only support was her daughter, then aged four, who became her care attendant, cook and cleaner. Little Emma is now very precocious and demanding of attention from anyone with whom she comes into contact.

DOROTHY LINCOLN

Dorothy lives in the North-East of England and cared for her increasingly disabled husband when she was in her forties and fifties. Following his death she continued to care for her mother and two aunts.

What the life of a carer is like

There is a saying that no one is indispensable but a carer (using the word in the sense meant by the Association of Carers) really can feel indispensable to her dependent relative. Indispensable in enabling a person who is diminished by illness to continue to live at home.

What does it feel like to be a carer? Well every situation is different, given that it involves different people each of whom is unique, just as every marriage is different, or every bereavement is different. Like these two examples it can be a personal, intensely felt experience but unlike them it is not such a common experience and certainly it is not so well documented. For me, caring for my husband when he became physically disabled and mentally confused was a rewarding experience.

On the debit side I felt grief at the sadness of the situation and I felt strain in coping with the demands on my strength and patience. But on the credit side it felt good to be able to meet the challenge. It was fulfilling to feel so necessary. I return to the word indispensable. For example an invalid who can no longer speak much but who can still understand and remember, needs a carer who knew him well before.

Being a carer in this context is not like being a nurse or a doctor. Professional carers have their limits defined and of necessity they should not get too involved. Although they may be very, very necessary they are always replaceable. They should not allow themselves to become indispensable. A professional nurse does not return to her patient in off-duty time to perform a service like letter writing. Professional home helps undertake such a wide range of services that they must sometimes feel extremely involved but they too have their hours of duty and holiday replacements.

One of the great plus factors in my situation was that my husband's essential nature did not change. I believe it sometimes happens that by reason of brain damage a personality change can occur. Some tensions and frustrations are inevitable but if a dependent relative really 'turned against' his carer that would be very difficult to bear.

Another psychologically helpful factor was that I felt satisfied that we had had the best medical opinion. Thereafter the situation was largely a nursing, caring one but I felt confidence in the diagnosis and prognosis. I was not agonising for a cure. My whole ambition was to find ways of easing the home scene and thereby keeping my husband at home in familiar surroundings, with as much comfort and dignity and security as could be arranged.

Practical aids were very important. About the most important was the telephone, especially in the early stages. To get help one must be able to communicate. One helpful contact may lead to another. Help comes from many different sources. Visits by doctor and nurses are not enough; to ask for things one has to know what is available. I was fortunate in that I was sufficiently young and strong to be persevering, and sufficiently confident and knowledgeable to be articulate, but I can well imagine that a carer could be quite trapped in her situation. It amazed me to find how a single aid (for example a small convenient bath hoist) could transform a bad situation into something manageable. I know that many caring relatives do not get such help.

Likewise a few minutes' instructions from a physiotherapist on how to get a disabled person to stand up from a sitting position made a world of difference to us. It saved my back, it helped my husband's self-esteem and it took the doubt and tension out of the manoeuvre. This particular help was never forthcoming from the doctor or nurse or occupational therapist. Workers tend to stay within their own disciplines. As I say, help comes from many different sources. I feel pleased to hear about and ready to support such a self-help action group as the Association of Carers.

It is over four years now since my husband died, so my memories have mellowed a little, but it was a challenge willingly accepted and it was rewarding. Now I am in a very different caring situation involving my mother and two aunts. We all live in separate houses in the same area of town. They have the usual complement of old age infirmities and two of them are housebound unless taken out by car. They receive a little practical help from the social services but I am the only 'young' relative around to do a multitude of jobs. Their neighbours are increasingly reluctant to help except in an emergency.

My present situation is nothing like as physically demanding as caring for my husband, but it is very wearing mentally and spiritually. I ponder and fret about why this should be and it helps temporarily to let off steam and talk about details even though this does nothing to improve the essential situation. I know that things could be much worse. I also believe that they could be much better.

Physical problems have practical solutions like hearing-aids or bath hoists, but psychological, personality problems are difficult to discuss and define let alone resolve. It is not 'just life'; it is a special section of life. Why are some elderly people so difficult? There are books for parents on child psychology. Are there useful books for daughters and sons about the psychology of elderly parents?

A few carers embrace their elderly relatives wholeheartedly, and some escaped carers reject them utterly until the funeral. Most people try to follow a mid-course between these two extremes. More guidance to travellers along this compromise path would be welcome.

PHYLLIS SCOTCHER

Phyllis is fifty-nine and lives on a large new estate in Woolwich. She is involved in Age Concern and also works for her local community. She is the mother of three and grandmother of four.

For half of my fifty-eight years I have been caring for my husband John, who is now sixty-three. He is a chronic arthritic; every joint in his body is affected. He is six feet three inches tall and weighs about fourteen and a half stone. We had been married seventeen months when Peter was born, John was fit at that time. He entered hospital for the first time when Peter was six months old; he was to stay there for six months. The doctors could not tell me what John's illness was and I remained in ignorance for nearly a year. His weight dropped from twelve and a half stone to seven and a half stone; he was in a dreadful state.

At this time our living conditions were very bad, just two rooms on the second floor of a very old house, no inside sanitation, no water in the house or even a sink. We just could not find anywhere else to live; life was very grim. I was unable to work and benefits in those days were very poor. My relations cared for my children (I had a daughter by a previous marriage) whilst I visited John. I was so desperately worried, they would not let him home until our living conditions improved. We were rehoused by the London County Council and two weeks later John came home. He had twenty bed sores which had to be dressed twice a day, we had no wheelchair and he could not walk, his legs had drawn up and he was in agony. I stood in the kitchen and wondered how on earth I was going to manage. I had always been pretty strong, so I was not worried about lifting, but I knew I could not carry him. So I put four castors on a dining room chair, and now I was able to push him into the bedroom.

The children were very good, they seemed to understand. There were always new problems, Peter needed new shoes, I had to ask for help and was sent to a well-known charity for second-hand shoes. They tried to squeeze his feet into a smaller size because his feet were large for his age – that was against the rules! I did manage to get him new shoes – I never asked again!

I managed to get a place in a nursery for Peter, Carol was at school, and I got a job as a crossing lady. It took two weeks to discover that I was worse off financially. I could not afford to work even though it was only a matter of about fifty pence, so I resigned. John's condition was deteriorating. We both knew it and we were very sad when he returned to hospital again. He was to stay there for nine months, for me a very worrying and sad time.

We had a dreadful experience at this time, it was the winter of 1955, a gas main had burst under our bedroom window, the three of us were almost unconscious when saved by some workman. This had really frightened me, and our doctor suggested we move; he said the flat was unsuitable now. We moved into our new home which we thought we would settle down in, John came home but he had not improved very much. I had been told he had rheumatoid arthritis, so at least I knew now what was wrong with him. He was so very cheerful considering the pain he suffered. All the months of waiting for his return, of the hours of visiting, were forgotten. There was a new worry looming, he was eating hardly anything, was always tired and he had a cough, then he coughed up spots of blood – he had tuberculosis. He had had it for some time, the doctor said, but as he was on cortisone it had been masked. I was shattered and so afraid for the children. We were examined and X-rayed and declared clear, thank God, I thought. John was away this time for a year.

Peter was beginning to have the same symptoms six months later and it was discovered he too had TB. By this time I started to question as to whether there was a God and I am still feeling like that. Peter was only two and a half years old. I kept thinking *why?* He went into hospital in Kent and was to stay for six months, so now I was visiting two hospitals, John's every day and Peter's twice a week – that was all I was allowed. I had to give Carol as much time as I could too. I remember in those days I had one dress which I had to wash overnight, one coat, one pair of shoes, my underclothes although clean were sewn and patched – we were really hard up.

John had an operation on his legs during his stay. They straightened them, and he was able to walk with the aid of crutches. It was a very painful business. He can still only walk about twenty-five yards. This we feel now was a mistake as it has made life very difficult.

We moved yet again and were settled in a week before John came home and Peter just after. We now lived in a pre-fab. It was very comfortable all on one level.

It was hard work adjusting to caring again. Peter was very

demanding; he wanted his Mum's attention, hook or by crook he was going to get it, so we battled on. Peter is now twenty-eight and married and when he comes to see us he follows me and still wants my attention. He was scarred by that absence from home. Things did improve slowly. John's army association sent us for a holiday – our first for five years. It was great to see the kids by the sea enjoying themselves; I still had to do the caring but it was a change which I enjoyed. We had a wheelchair now acquired for us by a friend at the cost of two and six pence a week, which made life a lot easier.

Out of the blue one day, we had a letter to say that the pre-fabs were to be demolished so we had to move again. We decided that the children must have a garden so we asked for a house. We felt sure we could work out a way of getting up the stairs, so we moved into a nice little house. The stairs were a problem, but after some trials and errors we managed it, John used one gutter crutch and me! We went up sideways, me first pulling him up slowly. This was to go on for fourteen years, during this time I damaged my wrist and several times slipped a disc. We found several ways of helping ourselves. We had to – there was no social services in those days, no aids at all were given to us.

Everytime my back gave out I had to continue to care for John, still getting up and down the stairs with him. I had to have a couple of operations, removal of my gall bladder and then two years later a hysterectomy. Each time my husband had to come into hospital as well. It was nice to see him at visiting times but it used to upset and worry me. I could see the little personal things were not being attended to. When it was time to go home John was sent home too, so caring started as soon as I got home. I had periods of depression and started to wonder how much more I could take, but of course one does carry on, trying to ignore any emotions that come over you.

We now live in a bungalow designed for the disabled. It is very nice, but councils make an awful lot of mistakes. I suppose this is how they learn. This bungalow is with four others in a row. The idea was to attract the people in the community to us, but in fact it has done just the opposite; we have very little contact with neighbours.

I am slightly handicapped myself now, although I still care for my husband. I should love a holiday on my own. Now I have written that I at once feel guilty. This is just one of the emotions which has bothered me. There is anger, I have felt cheated, ashamed, have loved and hated him. I have felt his frustrations, acknowledged his pain, but most of all I have loved him and have compassion for him.

I think of all the things I have missed most as fun, which we had so much of before he was sick. Life is so serious now. We have had lots of laughs even so.

I look forward to my children and grandchildren's visits very much, we have fun then.

There is no reward for being a carer, only the satisfaction of a job well done. I do realise that I am lucky that my husband is still alive. I shall be very lonely without him if he should die first, which is what I hope will happen but not for a long time yet.

I love watching seagulls flying. I can feel their freedom – maybe I will feel it one day.

During the last year I have been a member of a carers group. I find this now is an important part of my life. I have found friends in the same position as myself. We understand each other's problems and help each other if it is possible and we enjoy each other's company socially.

Susan F. has a handicapped son of nine years old. He is disabled both mentally and physically and requires frequent hospitalisation for various illnesses and operations. Mrs F's father, who lives with her and her husband, is becoming increasingly senile, demanding constant attention. He can only be quietened by riding in the car and Mrs F. often spends four or five hours a day just driving him around the area.

When her son next needed to go into hospital, the local authority told her that they had no Part III beds available to take her father whilst she accompanied her son. The child had to go into a distant hospital without his mother's support, as she had to remain at home with the old gentleman.

LILIAN MCSWEENEY

Lilian, divorced and in her fifties, cares for her elderly mother. She has two grown-up sons and was an active volunteer for many organisations including the Probation Service and Meals on Wheels before her caring responsibilities took over.

I was more than a little bemused when asked to join the Association of Carers. Someone at last had acknowledged the army of chain bearers. Until now, no one had shown interest and one was left to scream and rant and rave on one's own. In my own case I seem to have been a carer forever, having brought up two boys on my own. At that time I took on a part-time job to care for them and see to their needs. When they eventually established themselves, I decided to start afresh and to change my way of life. Living on maintenance and small income had been difficult.

Change came in a devastating way. My father died suddenly. Mother, who had been depressed previously, took his death badly. Her health worsened. She lived some distance away and the family – I have two brothers and sister – and I decided she must move nearer to us all. I managed to get her a flat nearby, and because I live on my own, it was taken for granted I should do the caring.

Perhaps because of the upheaval and insecurity of moving,

Mother turned very possessive and demanding. She had been prescribed valium treatment for many years. I know now this had added to her ill health. Eventually with care and understanding she was weaned off the valium and her health improved, although her hearing and eyesight did not. This makes life much more difficult for us both.

Mother has had five falls. Each time I have had the trauma of finding her sprawled across the floor having lain there for as long as two hours. I shudder to think how long she could have lain there had I not checked on her welfare regularly. Following one of the falls, mother became incontinent. Her bedding and clothing had to be changed frequently. I found the soiling difficult to cope with. I heaved and retched. That upset my mother no end. I asked the doctor if a nurse could come and assist me. She came daily, which eased things considerably. It gradually dawned on me that my life had become more and more centred around my mother. I realised with horror that I was a clock watcher. Whatever I might want to do had to be disregarded to meet her needs. I looked for support and found none. My mother relied solely on myself.

As mother's health improved, mine deteriorated. My nerves and body were crying out for a rest. I realised I didn't walk anymore, I ran. Friends remarked on my weight loss and careworn look. My own housework was neglected, my interests were falling by the wayside. The routine frustrated me, the frustration angered me. I tried to tell mother and the family I needed a break, this was met with the stinging remarks, I had brought her here and had regretted doing so. I will never regret giving my mother a new lease on her life but the process is very wearying. She says she cannot do without me.

One Saturday morning in sheer desperation, I visited an emergency doctor and poured out the anguish within me. Ironically he prescribed valium to help me through the weekend. I swallowed one immediately, walked slowly home and spent the rest of the day in a state of numbness. Later that evening I went to Mother's to find her in bed where she stayed for six weeks, refusing food. That meant more constant care. Specialists were called in. They prescribed massive doses of vitamins, given by injections. She was soon well and up again.

One day, on one of her visits, nurse suggested I get in touch with the 'Carers Support Scheme'. I did and the leader of the group visited me and explained how if I needed a couple of hours to myself she would send a member of her group to look after Mother. I was thrilled. At last I had some form of support.

I haven't had a holiday in many years, so, I was delighted when the Social Services offered to accommodate my mother in an hotel for the elderly to give me some sort of rest. Unfortunately she refuses any changes. Recently I attended my son's wedding, in London. To manage this I solicited the help of a nurse, a voluntary carer, two friends, the home help, my sister-in-law and a neighbour to do my duties over the weekend. Needless to say, I still left in a state of turmoil.

On my own accord I contacted the Social Services to ask for aids for my mother. They have provided her with many helpful furnishings and gadgets to make life easier. The health visitor organised a bath attendant to visit once fortnightly and a chiropodist every three months. I am more than grateful for this assistance. Mother is unable to do much, other than sit in a chair. She has only partial sight in one eye and is completely blind in the other. She is very deaf. One has to shout to be heard. Regular visits are essential. At times she gets querulous and upset at the lack of visits from her family, other days she makes excuses for them, saying they have to work and haven't the time to call. She doesn't accept that I work full days caring for her. The lack of support has more or less alienated me from the family.

My day normally begins when I rise at 7.15 a.m. After washing and dressing I have a cup of coffee and arrive at Mother's for 8 a.m. (No lie-in ever.) I make what little breakfast she wants and see to her immediate needs. I then do shopping. From then on, it is a case of anything I need to do for myself is done between calling in on Mother. An immediate need may be trivial but essential. Summer or winter my last call is around 10 p.m. to check she hasn't fallen while using the toilet. When I say my day normally starts at 8 a.m. that wasn't so when she was bed-bound and incontinent Then my day started at 5.30 a.m. and I was there all day until midnight. Lifting and changing mother is extremely painful for me. I suffer with cervical spondylitis and I am advised not to lift or carry.

My social life is practically non-existent. I rely heavily on friends visiting me. I know that life is passing me by and I cannot get a grip on it. Some days I feel that I am a leading figure in a full-blown drama, upstaged only by my mother and those around are the supporting cast taking minor roles and temporary parts. Other days I'm the lonely clown trapped in a circus knowing there is another way of life on the outside but unable to escape and participate. When I look to the future I quell the panic within. I am resigned to the fact there is no way out. One day the caring will cease; the rigid routine will stop. What then? Will it be too late to build anything at all for myself? Will I be capable and able? If not, then who will care for the carer?

Conclusion

After reading the contributions from the carers, one is left with the feeling that only a Dickens could do justice to the stories they tell. Poor housing, poverty, lack of understanding on the part of those whose job it is to advise and assist and a feeling of desolation and hopelessness among many, would have been the stuff of a novel for him. Where there is cheerfulness and a looking forward, it is in the face of adversity, not in the absence of it.

Many professional workers have said over the last three years, 'Oh, no! Not another client group!', but this totally misses the point. Carers have always been with us, just as have battered children, one-parent families and people with mental handicaps, but it takes a crisis to bring them to our attention. Policies of care in the community, combined with reductions in the level of support provided by statutory sources to families and demographic changes, have led to just such a crisis and brought the deprivations of carers to the forefront. One cannot then say that there are no resources to meet this 'new' group's needs, any more than one would refuse to protect a child at risk or leave a mentally handicapped person to beg on the streets. Indeed, there can be little excuse for any policy-makers not to have realised what the reality of twenty-four-hours-a-day care is. Many MPs' wives, government ministers' mothers and sisters, will have been carers or are caring at the moment and the contributors are describing events which have taken place over the last twenty or more years and five changes of government.

It is well illustrated by the carers here that merely keeping a disabled or elderly person alive is considered by many professionals to be the epitome of success. No thought is given to the continued care, well-being and quality of life of the carer and dependant. Many carers are asking that their dependants are not only kept in the world but are considered thereafter to be the joint responsibility of professionals, 'the community' and their families. 'Shared care', a phrase which is bandied around with increasing frequency, is seldom a reality. How can disabled people and their families be a part of the community, not apart *from* it?

There is a strong suspicion that keeping carers in ignorance of benefits and services is used as a rationing device. The Association of Carers receives many requests for help in the course of a year and finds it very distressing to be the one to inform a carer of a service available in her own area. This is likely to be a carer in contact with some form of statutory worker, if only the GP, and yet the help has not been made known to her. Another frequent example is of the lack of information provided on benefits from either the Department of Health and Social Security or other supposedly informed sources. Is this to keep costs down, or as simple a fact as the ignorance of the professional workers about what is available? In either case it is reprehensible that the information is not available to the people who need it. So the first request for improvement is a method of bringing the required information speedily to those who can benefit from it. It has been suggested in some quarters that a 'key worker' scheme may help; others believe that an extension of the Disablement Information and Advice Line (DIAL) system to all areas may be the answer. In truth, the solution may differ from area to area, but if the result is achieved, all well and good. If it is difficult to care in ideal circumstances, how much more so when there is a failure to provide the equipment and cash that could make life a little easier. Ease of access to information could go some way to making life more tolerable and ensuring that families have the resources to join in the life of the community.

The second part of the equation which might produce genuine 'shared care' lies in the provision of a range of services and support which can be tailored to suit all circumstances. There is a frequent complaint from carers that their right to relief is in the hands of the dependant. (Ruth writes graphically of her mother's refusal to go into residential care while she herself took a break, as does Doreen.) The usual response of a doctor or social worker to this situation is to say, with varying degrees of regret, 'I'm afraid I can do no more. Your mother/father/wife/husband refuses to go away.' It is very seldom, however, that the dependant is saying that they are refusing to be cared for by anyone else, even for a short time. This is the key to the success of the Crossroads Care Attendant Scheme, that the service is provided *within* the home, thereby reducing an understandable fear of the unknown to the minimum. Carers also say that the constant removal of an elderly person in particular from a familiar setting to one which is strange to them is the cause of increased confusion and a reduction in mobility. However, many carers do feel that they need time to spend in the home by themselves and then good and *acceptable* residential care can be the answer. At present, the standards of care are sometimes so low that, on the dependant's return home, the carer says 'never again'.

The range of options presently available nationwide (though not all by any means in any one area) would appear to be as follows:

Residential care (long-term)
Not usually seen as a viable proposition, as the vast majority of carers do wish to care for their relative at least part of the time. This can be from a sense of love or duty or (a common reason among the middle-aged or older) because of a 'death-bed' promise made to a parent.

Residential care (short-term)
Sometimes very useful, especially for annual holidays or at times of illness on the part of the carer, when she is unable

to undertake even part of her caring tasks, but can, as seen above, lead to perceived rapid deterioration in the dependant's condition. Usually it is far less acceptable to spouse than to daughter carers. The parents of disabled children, particularly the mentally handicapped, often press for this type of respite care. Because the quality of any form of residential care can vary so much, this form of help can be acceptable when the home is of a high standard but be totally unacceptable when the dependant returns, immobile and with pressure sores, both conditions forming a large number of complaints received by the Association. This type of care could be more useful if it was more immediately available – usually the booking has to be made well in advance.

Hospital rotating bed schemes
These are found far more frequently in geriatric wards than in any other type of medical provision and are less than enthusiastically received, except in an acute emergency or when the carer sees a full medical and para-medical assessment as being useful.

Foster care with families
These, once again, cause a certain amount of controversy. Many carers feel that such schemes cater only for the more active elderly, understandably, since the expense of converting the foster-home to the needs of, say, a frail person who uses a wheelchair all the time would be seen as inappropriate by most local authorities. However, carers see the comparatively 'untroublesome' elderly going away to give their families a break whilst the severely physically handicapped and the most floridly demented are left at home for their families to cope with unaided.

There is also a great deal of resentment about the payments which are made to foster families, which vary from about £40 a week in some areas to £100 in others. Many carers say that this seems unfair when their own care of their disabled or elderly relatives can actually cost them more than this, when one adds up lost earnings, additional heating and expensive forms of transport. The Disablement Income Group estimated (1984) that the cost to a family of having a mentally handicapped child is just under £4,000 a year, twice the cost of rearing an able-bodied son or daughter. A similar equation can be made with the care of an adult disabled person.

Care attendance schemes

The first of these, the Crossroads Care Attendant Scheme, set the pattern back in 1974. Broadly, the schemes offer a trained care attendant (*not* a trained nurse) to step in and relieve the carer at the time of day or night when help is required. They are highly spoken of by those carers who have access to them, the only criticism being that the majority of schemes are unable to offer more than a few hours' respite at a time. This is because of financial constraints (the schemes are usually part joint-funded and part privately fund-raised) rather than any philosophy of the organisation. Some carers say that they also require time in their home alone, rather than just the opportunity to go out and leave their dependant in the house with a care attendant.

Day care (in day centres or as a day patient in a residential home)

Day care which genuinely covers a whole working day can be vital in enabling the carer to keep on working, but frequently the 'day' is as little as four hours. Whilst this can be useful in leaving the carer to her own devices for a short time, the vagaries of the transport provided, which often cannot guarantee a definite arrival and return time, can cut even this brief period even further, as the carer has to be back home before the very earliest possible return of the vehicle, just in case. There are also complaints that many centres only care for the least disabled, turning down elderly people who are prone to wander, or physically handicapped people who require assistance in using the lavatory, for example.

Night centres

A very new phenomenon, night centres pick up their clients in the evening and return them home the next morning. These are very much appreciated in the very few places they exist, since they offer the carer the opportunity to have an uninterrupted night's sleep, enabling her to cope more efficiently with the stresses of the day. They are extremely helpful, too, to the carer with other responsibilities, leaving her free to go out with her husband or to spend time with her children when they come in from school. It has been remarked that night care is the solution to the problem of changes in circadian rhythms, which sometimes occur in conditions such as Alzheimer's disease.

Community Nursing Service

The general consensus is that the community nursing service is of considerable help at times when the dependant is acutely ill or post-operative but is not to be seen as a means of obtaining respite, since the nurse expects the family carer to be in the house when she arrives and frequently requires the help of the carer for tasks like lifting, which nurses are not allowed to undertake by themselves (though the carer is seldom aided in this!). It seems that the nursing service itself is not entirely sure what its precise purpose is; some nurses do see themselves as relieving the carer of some tasks; others believe that their role is to teach the carer how to undertake these tasks and then to withdraw. A major difficulty is imposed by the usual timing of the service – something like 7.30 a.m.-5.30 p.m. – which is of little use when the dependant must be up at 7.00 a.m. or cannot go to bed before 10.00 p.m. in order not to risk pressure sores from lying on one side for too long. The most common help received is in once-weekly or fortnightly assistance with bathing. Where there is a Nurse Continence

Adviser, she is held in high regard, as little is on offer in most areas in the event of incontinence except a supply of incontinence pads.

Home Help Service
This service is very little offered to carers, unless they themselves are frail or disabled. Several carers have said that it is not a very relevant service, as it is extremely difficult to get themselves organised to fit in with the times that the home help comes – perhaps their dependant went to sleep and they were able to do their housework an hour before the home help was due to arrive one day, but were in the middle of getting them up the next. Also, they often take a pride in producing a 'nice home' and enjoy shopping as a means of going out of the house, both the traditional tasks taken on by the home help service.

Where there are augmented schemes offering more than this, the service is usually seen as one for keeping elderly people out of residential care, and is hence directed at the elderly living alone. Such services are seldom seen as a way of offering a relief to the carer.

This may have painted a rather gloomy picture of the services available, or made carers out to be an ungrateful lot – neither of these were intended. The aim was to show that for every service which is provided, there will be those for whom it is the answer to their prayers and others to whom it will be of no help at all, and a variety of options should be available in every area.

Emotional stresses

The aim was not either to say that the answer to all caring problems lies in providing respite services, important as they are. Any support to carers must take into consideration the psychological and emotional stresses which accompany the subjugation of self. It is not surprising that many carers are the first to acknowledge that their experience has damaged them in some way. Some speak of total lack of confidence and the inability to express their own needs, even when an offer is made; some feel completely isolated from their peers, 'on another planet' as one put it, and this is a danger sign for the beginnings of psychiatric illness; others complain that they are 'neutered', sexless and unsure of their value to anyone other than in their servitude. Counselling, both into and out of caring, is rarely available and, where it is, is frequently seen as a way of 'making them carry on caring' (for fiscal reasons, usually). Carers' support groups can be of value, a forum for carers to speak their minds on their situations, but anyone who has tried to run one will be aware of the difficulties of persuading carers to come there in the first place. This can be because it is genuinely difficult to find a substitute whilst they go out, but also because time spent on themselves can be seen as frivolous in their own eyes.

Carers speak so often of 'being in second place', 'putting their own needs last' and so on, and it is easy to see that this self-denigration, loss of self-esteem and effacement is a concomitant of the caring role. If the carer has never had any attention paid to her needs and has had to carry on tending even when she herself is ill or would wish to be elsewhere, the end result is that she is a doormat, without ability to assert her own personality and make choices for herself. In the end, even the most normal of desires, for privacy, self-determination and respite, can seem to both dependant and carer as selfish and uncaring.

A common fallacy is that the experiences of caring are similar to those of 'normal' child-rearing, and indeed there are shared problems – isolation, low income, lack of sleep. But the solutions are usually much easier for the mother to find than the carer of an adult dependant, or even of a severely disabled child. Whilst the young mother can put the baby in the pram and go to visit a friend or go for a walk into town, this option is seldom available to the carer. How does one persuade the disabled husband to come in his wheelchair to the Mothers' Union coffee morning? Or cope with the demented old lady in the Wimpy Bar? How much more strength and energy does one need to push thirteen stone in a wheelchair weighing another two stone at least? And what about the bedridden?

The most important difference, however, is that of time-scale. The parent looks forward to the child leaving home, becoming independent, perhaps marrying. This is how parental success is measured and is the reward for years of caring and loving. The carer of a person with a disability can only see her task ceasing on the death of either her or her dependant, and this can bring with it the most crippling guilt. The equation is 'I wish to be free. I will only be free when you die. Therefore I am wishing you dead.' To care for twenty, thirty, fifty years is now not uncommon. Members of the Association are of all ages from sixteen to ninety-nine. Some of the young ones may now be facing fifty years of loss of self in another's needs, many of the older have already completed the half-century.

Inviting friends in is seldom the answer, either. Unlike small children who can be left with the playbox while their mothers chat, there is little likelihood of two adult dependants being so easily amused. Common courtesy demands that they are included in the conversation and many a carer of a person who is less than lucid has told of the embarrassment this can cause at times, or of the elderly person who hogs the conversation with long stories of people and places not known to anyone else in the company. One carer described the difficulty of having friends round when she always had to check the bathroom before anyone went in, to clean away any smeared faeces, and the sadness when her family would no longer eat together because of the appalling table manners of their grandfather.

An incidental issue here is that carers usually have to host family gatherings because of the difficulty of using transport or of staying in a home which cannot accommodate the disabled dependant, which precludes staying with other members of the family. The expense of Christmas, for example, is usually very high, as all the children, grandchildren and friends will have to come to the carer's house, and she will be exhausted afterwards.

Family support

This leads on to the issue of support from other members of the family. A common story is of all other members of the family unit fading away and leaving all the work and responsibility to one person. This leads to enormous bitterness and resentment. It would be an interesting area of research to find out why some people become carers, whilst others not only do not, but do not even contemplate it. Why does one daughter take on the full-time care of a parent, for example, and the others see that job as being nothing to do with them? There is sometimes a fairly obvious reason – one daughter lives in the next street whilst the other is in Australia – but this is by no means always the case.

There will always be some families who try to share the load and this can work well in some cases. However, desirable as this may be as a concept to the state, it seems that statutory authorities who are actually responsible for providing support services do little to encourage it. To give an example, an elderly lady, already a little confused, was knocked down by a car and thereafter required considerable help in the home and with all aspects of personal care. Her three children, one in the South-East, one in the Midlands and the third in the Home Counties, agreed that they would have her to live with them for four months of the year each. When the first applied to her local authority for adaptations to the home, she was refused, on the grounds that her mother was 'not a permanent resident' in the authority's area. Her mother was denied a bus-pass on the same grounds and could never put her name down for the day centre, since the waiting list was so long that she would have been with the next daughter before it came to the top. The same applied four months later, when she moved on, and each of the children was involved in a great deal of personal expenditure, just because they were behaving like a loving and caring unit.

The question of the carer's support of *other* members of the family is one which is seldom raised. Care in the community is sold on the premise that it is a measure which keeps families together and encourages us to look after our own. However, it is usually impossible for a carer to look after more than one person or household satisfactorily. Ruth describes the difficulties in apportioning her time and attention to both her mother and her husband and children, and Pat's father died in hospital, because his daughter could not bring him home to nurse him for the last few days, as well as giving her mother the attention she demanded and needed.

As carers approach middle-age, they feel very resentful that they are unable to support their adult children through childbearing and rearing or to give the help they would wish to their ageing parents because they already are fully occupied in looking after a disabled spouse or handicapped child. So what might at first seem to be an economically attractive proposition appears less so when one considers that a full range of community services will be called upon to support the 'neglected' relative. If assistance was given to all parties, the family could make up the difference with little difficulty. Because the 'all or nothing' policy prevails, the carer is utterly tied to one person and is unable to make even a modest contribution to the care of others in her immediate family circle.

Environmental restrictions

The environment, about which we have heard far more in the last decade, can be the single most important factor in making caring successful or not. If the home in which caring is being undertaken is totally unsuitable for the disabled person, that person will be unable to do many things which would be appropriate for their level of handicap. In other words, many people are restricted, not by the extent of their impairment, but by the setting in which they have to cope with it. Every task which the environment precludes the dependant from doing is one more task for the carer to do. Practical examples of this are: kitchens which are inaccessible and therefore deny the dependant the opportunity to make a drink or learn to cook and wash-up; bathrooms and lavatories so unsuitable that the disabled person always has to be accompanied and assisted; thresholds with steps or too-steep ramps, meaning that unaided access is impossible. So often one feels that adaptations and improvements are denied to a disabled person when an able-bodied carer is there to make good the deficiency. The attitude seems to be 'it doesn't matter that Mr X can't get into the kitchen, his wife will do all the cooking', forgetting that Mrs X cannot return to work if her husband is without food or drink all day, and ignoring Mr X's frustration at having to wait for his wife to do something which he is physically capable of doing himself. For whose benefit is this?

Another way in which the environment disables is when access is denied to the disabled who cannot be left alone at home. If the local High Street is impossible to negotiate and if the dependant is unsafe in the house without supervision, then the carer is just as restricted as if she herself was wheelchair bound. One carer who wrote to the Association was in the position of not having left her flat for two years. Her mother had had both legs amputated and could no longer go up or down the eight steps to their home. Because of this, her daughter had to do all the shopping by telephone. They had their name down for alternative suitable premises for over five years.

Caring and work

Many carers are forced to give up work entirely when

disability strikes. This is a multiple tragedy. It means that they no longer have an income, or status, or a legitimate reason for leading a life of their own, and when the caring is over, it is well nigh impossible for most of them ever to return to the work-force.

Financially, there is only one benefit to which carers are entitled if they cease paid employment, the Invalid Care Allowance (ICA), but at the time of writing, that is only payable to men and to single women, married and cohabiting women being regarded as in receipt of support from their husbands or cohabitees. This rule applies no matter for whom they are caring. There is an ongoing campaign to have this position changed, but it would appear to be a low priority for all political parties.

If a carer is entitled to supplementary benefit in his or her own right, the iniquitous 'voluntarily unemployed' rule applies. This states that if a person voluntarily removes him/herself from work, supplementary benefit will be reduced by 20 per cent for the first six weeks of the claim, and incredibly, giving up work to care for a severely handicapped relative counts as 'voluntarily' relinquishing employment.

All these regulations make it extremely difficult for carers to protect both their current income and their future pension rights. One way for a carer to have a class I national insurance credit awarded to count towards her pension is the same as the one which protects women bringing up under-16s – Home Responsibilities Protection (HRP). This awards NI credits to take account of years when women are out of the work force because of caring duties. However, it has failed to take notice of current thinking about caring, which says that regular respite is essential, since, if the dependant is away, in hospital, residential home, on holiday or staying with another member of the family, for five weeks or more during the course of a year (and a hospital admission plus the annual holiday can more than easily add up to this), the carer receives no NI credits for the *whole* of that year, not just for the periods of the dependant's absence.

There would certainly seem to be a case for 'carers' leave', a breathing space for the carer to find out what degree of recovery is going to be possible and to decide what the best course of action is going to be. As things are at the moment, a decision is often forced on the carer, by employer or medical profession, and subsequent events mean that this might not have been necessary. This situation most often arises after strokes and accidents. The disabled person appears at first to be in a condition which will necessitate permanent and substantial care, but a better recovery than was forecast is made and the loss of the job is proven to have been unnecessary.

It is a common occurrence for a carer who is not at work to give far more help to her dependant than is really necessary, just because she is there. A person left alone will often struggle to do something which he wants, but will just ask the carer to do it if she is present. Carers who have been able to continue to work frequently dread retirement, because they know that it will encourage the disabled person to become more dependent on them.

Coming back to the effects of lack of information, it is not unusual to find a carer giving a totally unrealistic level of care to a person whose needs have changed over the years. The medical and other professions fail to inform them as to what is required at a particular time and so the care given is kept at the level at which it was at the point of discharge from hospital. A regular assessment which includes the carer would obviate this unnecessary burden. This would also ensure that a carer was not mistakenly believing that her presence was essential and give her the chance to consider returning to employment when the care could be reduced to an acceptable minimum.

Carers are already doing at least three jobs – those tasks which they would normally undertake, those which their dependant would normally undertake and what amounts in many cases to a full-time nursing job – and it may to an observer appear strange that many wish to take on yet another

– outside employment. But for the reasons given above – contact with the outside world, status in society and legitimation of the need to get away from the claustrophobic atmosphere of twenty-four-hour-a-day servitude – every encouragement should be given by employers, medical and social work professionals and the employment services, to assisting those carers who wish to take on paid work to find a job which fits their situations.

Sexuality

A much-neglected issue is sexuality, and it is interesting to note that, with the exception of Anna, the only contributors to mention their sex-lives are the men.

Much has been spoken of disability and sexuality, but far less of the problems of being totally able-bodied and yet having either to relinquish one's sexuality or to adapt it to a degree which is found unacceptable by the individual. Whilst different postures or incomplete sex might be found to be adequate by a person who knows that that is all that is possible, they might not be so to the non-disabled partner, who knows that she personally could be leading a fuller and more 'normal' sex-life.

Even when it is not the sexual partner who is disabled, sexuality can be affected. One hears of the parents of handicapped children who are unable ever to go to bed at the same time, because one of them has to sit up with the child, or of elderly parents wandering in and out of the bedroom all night, or in one case, believing that her son was her late husband and regularly dragging him from that 'strange woman's' bed, the woman in question being her daughter-in-law. Not a situation conducive to a fulfilled sexuality, one would think.

Even the providers of statutory services often fail to acknowledge the needs of families in this respect, providing single bedroom extensions, single beds and no information about aids to sexuality.

Once the feeling of being a sexual person is gone, caring for a husband or wife can, as one woman put it, be merely a nursing or care attendant task. One becomes the 'arms and legs' of the dependant and love goes too. It is ironic that carers are often pushed into their task, or volunteer willingly for it, because they love the disabled person, but the circumstances of caring so frequently eventually kill love, replacing it with resignation or a sense of duty.

Even when there was little holding the relationship together before the onset of disability, there is a strong social feeling that it is 'not quite right' to leave a marriage where one partner is handicapped. Opprobrium will surely follow, from friends, family, professionals. Several carers who have contacted the Association have made comments about this, saying that they very much wish to end the marriage, but feel that it is somehow unfair to leave a person who is dependent on them for their needs, and very existence sometimes. One sees marriages turning into relationships which more closely resemble that of a parent and child, and yet there will always be the feeling that a marriage is a marriage.

Jimmy comments that he thinks that wives stay with disabled husbands more than husbands with disabled wives. This statement may not be scientifically proven, but one certainly has a subjective impression that this is the case. There is a strong feeling that a wife leaving a disabled husband would attract more adverse comment than a man.

Even more fundamental than sexuality and the opportunity to express it is the loss of feelings of gender. Even in these times of diminishing gender-roles, everyone still needs to feel that they are male or female, and this is something which is missing in the lives of many carers. Men speak of being emasculated, women of being defeminised – they appear to meet at a neutral central point. Again, research into this would be invaluable, as it is a factor which causes carers great distress. One woman telephoned the Association in tears. She had looked after her husband, who has had Alzheimer's disease, for sixteen years and has taken over the complete running of their lives, since her husband is mentally unable to think and make decisions. What had led to her eventual breakdown was that a man of her acquaintance had made a pass in a comparatively friendly and non-threatening way to her. She said that she had not realised until that moment how genderless she had become. She was as revolted by his action, she said, as she would have been by a homosexual approach.

Summary

Carers will always be with us. They will continue to care for the people close to them for eternity and they deserve far more than they are getting at the moment. The contributors to this book would no doubt be embarrassed were they to be praised sky-high and say they are only doing what is their duty, but this will never be a reason for neglecting them and more than a million others in the same situation and forcing them to go through the circumstances they so vividly describe.

If the situation seems bleak now, how much more so will it be when the full effects of changing policies and a diminishing ratio of carers to dependants are felt? At the turn of the century, there were seventeen women relatives to every person over the age of sixty-five. There are now fewer than three to every elderly person. The injured and sick are being kept alive but dependent, and these people will require life-long care from those same relatives who are trying valiantly to support their own parents. Put this with policy decisions which include earlier discharge from hospital, a vast increase in day surgery and a determination to keep retired people in their own homes, or those of a member of their family, and there is a tinder-box of resentment, anger and rebellion.

Caring is now out of the closet. Let us give it a good airing, shake it around a little and see if the garment can be adapted so that it actually fits those who take it on or have it thrust upon their shoulders.

If you've read this book, you might be interested in the following related Routledge titles:

Images of Ourselves: Women with disabilities talking: Edited by Jo Campling

'Could have been sub-titled "True Grit": any one of these 24 short autobiographies of girls and women afflicted with paralysis, blindness, epilepsy or palsy might draw horror, pity, amazement and admiration. Taken as a group, they make you question the categories we impose: who is the "normal person", the doctor who leads a group of medical students to prod and poke silently at an adolescent girl with cerebral palsy, or the same girl who painfully teaches herself to respect her own body, despite the doctor? An original and extraordinary book.' – Clare Tomalin, *The Sunday Times*, 19 April 1981

'Excellent book in which over 20 women with varied disabilities write informatively and movingly about their lives.' – Mary Sanford, member of Boston Women's Health Collective and co-author of *Our Bodies, Ourselves*, *Sojourner*, Cambridge, Mass.

'I didn't learn enough about disabilities from this fine book, but I did learn two important things: first, that so-called disability doesn't stop the process of living a life, and second, when it happens to me (even if only through old age, it *will* happen), I am not alone; these women provide models for me to take courage and strength from.' – Paige Cousineau, Women's Studies Group, Brussels, *Resources for Feminine Research*, Toronto, January 1984

A Labour of Love: Women, work and caring: Edited by Janet Finch and Dulcie Groves

'*A Labour of Love* offers a core of chapters on what the labour of caring *feels* like, drawing on the experiences of women caring for dependent disabled children, spouses and parents, drawing out the complicated relationship of emotional ties and the very real hard labour that can be involved in tending another's needs. . . . The whole book is a nicely balanced, readable, well edited collection, written by researchers with proven track records in their fields.' – Laura Middleton, *Social Work Today*, 1 November 1983

'Every day a silent army, an estimated 800,000-strong, fights to support handicapped children and adults, and chronically sick and frail elderly, outside residential accommodation. These women have been called on to put aside their own careers and aspirations to shoulder the responsibility of a dependant, with all this entails. . . . This book is a disquieting study undertaken by 10 contributors, each concerned with a specific aspect of caring, be it emotional, practical, social or economic.' – Julie Hand, *Nursing Mirror*, December 1983

Also

Unshared Care: Parents and their disabled children: Caroline Glendinning

The Costs of Caring: Families with disabled children: Sally Baldwin